¡Viva el Español!

¡HOLA!

TESTING PROGRAM

Blackline Masters

Stanley W. Connell
Martha Lucía Torres
Test Designers

Jean D'Arcy Maculaitis
Testing Specialist and Consultant

National Textbook Company
a division of *NTC Publishing Group* • Lincolnwood, Illinois USA

Acknowledgments

The publisher would like to thank the students from Holy Cross School, Rumson, New Jersey, and Our Lady of Perpetual Help School, Highlands, New Jersey, who participated in the pilot test for the *¡Viva el español!* testing program. Thanks also to Dr. Kay Hampares, an internationally renowned expert on the Spanish language and culture, who worked on a pilot experiment in Florida, and to Dr. Jean D'Arcy Maculaitis, a second-language teaching and testing specialist, who conducted the pilot studies.

To the Teacher:

The blackline masters in this book are designed to be photocopied for classroom use only.

Published by National Textbook Company,
a division of NTC Publishing Group
4255 West Touhy Avenue
Lincolnwood (Chicago), Illinois 60646–1975 U.S.A.

Manufactured in the United States of America.

67890 VL 987654321

CONTENTS

STUDENT TESTS (BLACKLINE MASTERS)

End-of-Year Test   106

INTRODUCTION

Assessment and evaluation of progress in acquiring a second language play an important part in sustaining students' enthusiasm for language learning, and offer you vital feedback necessary for tailoring your teaching to the needs of individual learners. In second-language learning, because students are constantly being asked to produce responses or react to communicative stimuli, there are frequent opportunities for assessment. However, because of the nature of communication and language production, there are different strategies required for assessment and evaluation. The *¡Viva el español!* program offers you frequent, creative opportunities and ideas for carrying out these vital functions.

Types of Assessment

Assessment in second-language learning needs to operate at a number of different levels, because of the many layers of skills and proficiencies that are being acquired, and that thus need to be assessed and evaluated. The types of assessment fall into three major categories: proficiency, achievement, and prochievement. Furthermore, each of these categories can be assessed through both formal and informal means.

Proficiency Assessment

Since the goal of our language teaching is to develop communicative proficiency in students, we must find ways to assess that proficiency. Proficiency assessment seeks to determine what students can do with the language they've been acquiring, and to what extent they can transfer that language into real-life settings that require them to both receive and give information—the act of communication. The emphasis in proficiency assessment is on performance.

There is, however, a "slippery" quality to communication that can make assessment difficult at times. There is not always a "right" answer. For example, there may be countless ways in which a student could respond to a given question or situation, each of which is appropriate. Students may give you answers you don't expect, ones that may take you by surprise, but that still respond directly to the question or situation you've posed. Students may also give responses that are imperfect on a structural or fluency level, but that nevertheless communicate a message that is understandable and appropriate to the requirements of the setting. Proficiency must be looked at in a very global, holistic way. You must constantly ask yourself the question, "Did I understand the message the student was trying to convey?"—and you must remain open and flexible in assessing what your students produce.

You should be aware that proficiency assessment can be very time-consuming, because it requires interaction with individual students or groups of students. For this reason, you may want to spread your assessments out over the entire course of the lesson, working your way through the class. Don't worry that some students will have had more opportunity to prepare for the assessment because they've had additional days of instruction. Language proficiency is not delineated with clear milestones, but is instead an evolutionary, holistic process that does not change dramatically from one day to the next.

Achievement Assessment

Achievement assessment looks at what students know, rather than at what they can do. Unlike proficiency assessment, achievement testing generally has answers that are right or wrong, and is relatively objective. It requires students to demonstrate retention of previously learned content material. In the case of language learning, achievement assessment can tell you whether students have learned specific vocabulary items, for example, or whether they know accurate endings for a verb or an adjective. As such, it is much easier to set objectives and to evaluate progress in this area. Historically, this sort of assessment has been the mainstay of language testing. However, as our goals have changed, achievement testing has taken on less importance. It remains, however, an important part of the overall assessment of student progress.

Prochievement Assessment

Prochievement is a word that has been coined to describe a type of assessment that combines characteristics of both proficiency and achievement testing. It asks students to demonstrate what they know in a meaningful context. Where traditional achievement testing has asked students to respond to isolated items, prochievement testing ties the items together in some sort of situation. You are still asking students to tell you what they know, and there are still right and wrong answers, but you come much closer to simulating communicative use of language. Prochievement assessment may also allow students to respond within a *range* of correct answers—i.e., there might be two or three acceptable responses to an item, but still there is an objectively "right" way of answering. Many of the activities and exercises in the student book follow this model, and lend themselves to assessment opportunities.

Formal vs. Informal Assessment

Each of the categories listed above can be assessed either formally or informally. In the case of formal assessment, students generally should be made aware that they are being assessed, and also be given some opportunity to prepare. It is important to give formal assessments regularly, though not so frequently that they become burdensome to you or your students. Formal assessments tend to create a great deal of anxiety in many students, and while valuable, may in some cases actually hinder the learning process. You should try to help the students understand your goals in assessing them, and make efforts to lower the stress surrounding this sort of testing. Avoid comparing students directly. Create an atmosphere in which individual students see formal testing as something between you and them, designed to help them, rather than to rank them. Formal assessment should usually result in some sort of feedback to the learner concerning performance so that the assessment does not serve as an end in itself, but rather as a tool for aiding the learner in understanding and improving. Suggestions for scoring or otherwise quantifying performance on formal assessments are discussed later in this article.

Informal assessments can be entirely spontaneous, and may be carried out even without the students' awareness. This sort of assessment does not necessarily result in a score or quantifiable outcome, but will still provide much valuable information for both you and your students. Informal assessment should take place as frequently as practical. It may be as simple as taking note of individual, pair, or group oral performance on an activity as you walk around the room, or as you read over written activities, or look over drawings and posters that arise out of an activity. It might also be more intentional, coming at the end of a presentation or sequence of practice and taking the form of a special set of questions that you ask students to respond to or a brief task that you ask them to perform. Virtually any activity in the text will lend itself to informal assessment.

Assessment Strategies

There is virtually no limit to the strategies that can be used in evaluation of language proficiency and achievement. In fact, it could be argued that anytime students produce language, you have an occasion for assessment and evaluation. Each teacher will need to find his or her preferred strategies and techniques based on individual teaching goals and requirements. However, there are some general principles and strategies that will assist you in finding creative solutions for your assessment needs.

"Assessment Opportunity" Helps

Throughout the *Annotated Teacher's Editions* of *¡Viva el español!* you will find numerous suggestions labeled as "Assessment Opportunities." These appear in the Unit Plans section at the front of each book and in the on-page annotations for the student pages. As you read through them, you will find creative suggestions for using the material in the student book, or in some way going beyond it, to find out what your students are capable of, both in terms of proficiency and achievement. In many cases, we suggest ways to vary items from an exercise that students have just been working on. We also offer ideas for linking the practice to real-life events that your students can relate to. We might suggest a game that will use the vocabulary students are learning, or we might give you some questions to ask to elicit particular vocabulary items or structures. Here are just a few examples:

- Ask students to borrow something from a classmate. Have them display on their desks the borrowed item plus one that is their own. Circulate around the classroom, choosing one item of the two on a student's desk, and asking, **¿De quién es?**

- Call out the names of teachers in your school. Have students respond by stating the subject each one teaches.

- State the following situations in English and ask students to tell you what they would say, using an appropriate **tener** expression: 1. It's 99° outside and the air conditioner is broken. (**Tengo calor.**) etc.

- Have students write the answers to three items of their choosing from Ex. B. Let them exchange papers and correct one another's answers.

You should not look at the "Assessment Opportunities" as the only occasions for evaluation. Look at them as ideas, and glean from them strategies that you can apply in other settings.

One-on-One Assessment

Particularly with younger learners, it can be difficult to find time to isolate yourself with one student to perform one-on-one evaluation. It would be ideal to find ways to do this that would afford some measure of interaction with a single student while still allowing you to maintain control over the class as a whole. This will most often occur while the class is working on a task that requires some quiet time, such as working on a writing project. Call students over to a corner of the room with you one at a time, or stand next to their desks and talk quietly with them. A few times a year, you might arrange "special project" days to allow yourself the opportunity for formal assessment, planning to spend two or four minutes with each student, perhaps over the course of two days. Some teachers have also had success with calling students at home, or working with them at lunch or recess periods, or having them record responses on cassettes that the teacher then listens to outside of class.

In practice, much of your one-on-one evaluation will need to take place "on the fly," as you call on individual students to respond, or as you look over a student's written work. Be careful to give all students opportunities for responding to you individually. It is very easy for extremely verbal or extroverted students to dominate in a second-language class where the emphasis is on communication. Introverted students or those struggling with the language will need some special opportunities to interact with you without fear of embarrassment.

Group Assessment

Group assessment is most easily conducted by observing and monitoring activity while the group is performing a task. Be sure to circulate from group to group. As much as possible, you should avoid interfering in the process, allowing students to interact with one another and correct one another. Evaluate students on their participation in the overall process, as well as on their individual contributions. A second assessment opportunity then exists when the product of the task is presented to the class. The *Entre amigos* and *¡A divertirnos!* activities throughout the program provide excellent opportunities for assessing group performance.

Portfolio Assessment

A superb technique for evaluation over time is afforded by portfolio assessment. By having students create portfolios of written work and projects, you end up with a series of "snapshots" of progress that can demonstrate for you and for the student what has been achieved over time. Furthermore, you have a product that can be revised, expanded, and improved by the student as new language is acquired, allowing you to compare new production with the benchmark of the original. Portfolios are also useful for motivating and involving parents in the learning process as they review what their children have been doing.

Many of the *Entre amigos* and *¡A divertirnos!* activities call for students to produce written work, drawings, posters, greeting cards, etc., all of which can be used to create a portfolio. In many cases, the *Entre amigos* practice will even ask students to go back and add to work done for earlier activities, refining or supplementing. You will also find a number of suggestions for student-created Big Books that would lend themselves well to this sort of assessment.

Peer Assessment

When treated sensitively, peer assessment can be an extremely effective tool. Because so many of the activities in the *¡Viva el español!* program are designed for pair and group work, students quickly become used to working with partners, and become comfortable with being assessed by a peer. Among other ways, this can be accomplished by having partners look over one another's work and make editing changes or corrections, by having students prepare short quizzes for one another, or by having a student listen to another student and note down the information he or she hears, and then check it with the person who gave the information. You might ask students to call one another at home in the evening and share information in Spanish. The next day, they can compare what they heard with what the other student thinks was said, and report on the accuracy of the communication. You can also give students checklists of objectives and other criteria for evaluating an activity, and ask them to evaluate the work of their pair or group based on those criteria.

It is important that students understand clearly from the outset that no harshness or unkindness will be tolerated when assessing or correcting their classmates. You will need to create a climate of trust and a sense of classroom community that will minimize the sometimes critical nature of early adolescents.

Self-Assessment

Students benefit when they learn that evaluation is not entirely the teacher's responsibility, and when they learn the value of assessing their own work. Portfolios, mentioned above, are excellent vehicles for teaching the art of critical review of one's own efforts. When quizzes are given, you might provide answer keys on overhead transparencies and ask students to check their own work. You could also provide checklists of objectives before an activity begins and have students rate themselves on how they attain the objectives at the end of the practice. Use the list of objectives on the first page of each student unit as one such checklist. Just before the unit test, ask students to read over the objectives that were set out and ask themselves if they can do each of those things, now that they've gone through the unit. If they find there are things they don't know how to do, they should report this to you so you have an opportunity for reteaching. Self-assessment comes more easily to some students than to others, and will require some practice.

Evaluation and Scoring

While some assessment is entirely informal and requires no quantification, there is still a need for scoring or tracking your evaluations. Particularly with formal assessment, you probably have district or state requirements for reporting an evaluation. Even informal assessments can lose their value for you if you do not record them in some way. There are a number of means of scoring or otherwise recording evaluations. The Testing Program that supplements the series has its own scoring system. Below are some ideas for scoring the other assessments you carry out in class. No matter what system you use, however, we sometimes have a tendency to look at the scores as a means of ranking learners, of proving what they don't know. Evaluation is much more useful when we look at it as an indicator of what students *do* know.

Achievement Evaluations

Achievement and prochievement evaluations are the easiest to score. Because items are objectively right or wrong, you can readily assign point values and keep track of them in a grade book. If you wish to record results of informal prochievement or achievement assessments, you might consider making simple tick-marks beside students' names in your grade book or on index cards to indicate successful responses. These can be tallied weekly and assigned a value. If you are not opposed to the idea of tokens, you might keep a supply of paper money or plastic tokens at hand. Each time students respond correctly, hand them one of the tokens. At the end of the week, they can turn the tokens in, and you can record a score based on the number of tokens.

Proficiency Evaluations

Proficiency evaluation can be tricky, given the subjective nature of language and communication, the virtually infinite number of responses that can be given in many situations, and the fact that communication can occur even when a response is flawed. If there is not a right answer, how can we score performance? To effectively evaluate proficiency, we need to look at a larger set of criteria. One such set could look like this:

- Did the student complete the communicative task?

- Was the message that was conveyed appropriate?

- How creative was the response?

- Was the response linguistically accurate?

- Did the student find ways to express ideas in spite of language limits?

- Did the student perform at ability level?

- Was progress demonstrated?

These lists of criteria could vary according to your personal goals and preferences. Once a set of criteria is established, a rating scale can be created. Obviously, not every one of the criteria is as important to communication as the others. This then calls for a weighted scale which gives more points to those factors that most affect communication, or that combines factors while still giving the greatest weight to communication. A simple scale might look like this:

Score	Performance
5	Excellent communication, almost no errors
4	Communicated well, but with noticeable errors
3	Communicated fairly well, but with many noticeable errors
2	Response understandable, but grossly erroneous
1	Practically incomprehensible
0	No response

The ¡*Viva el Español!* Testing Program

A formal, self-contained assessment program accompanies each of the three textbooks in the ¡*Viva el español!* series. For each level the Testing Program includes the following components:

- Testing Program blackline master book containing a detailed description of the program, suggestions and instructions for testing, blackline masters of the tests, an answer key for all written and oral tests, a complete tapescript of the audio Test Cassette, and a Student Progress Chart.

- Test Cassette with listening-comprehension activities corresponding to the oral testing sections in the Testing Program.

The components have been designed bearing in mind that students react most favorably to materials that are appealing and applicable to real conversation and that you, as a teacher, need testing materials that are pedagogically sound and easy to prepare and score.

Evaluation Techniques

The evaluation techniques and design of the ¡*Viva el español!* Testing Program are compatible with the Natural Approach and Total Physical Response, approaches that stress the use of interesting and relevant materials, comprehensible input, and intense observation and involvement from students. The design of the Testing Program will help you create a nonthreatening testing environment in your classroom—an environment that allows sufficient success to encourage low to average achievers, yet stimulates high achievers and students who are gifted in second-language learning.

Test Types and Objectives

The ¡*Viva el español!* Testing Program features two types of tests: (1) a Placement Test to be administered at the beginning of the year and (2) Unit Tests.

Placement Test

At the beginning of the school year, your students will fall into one of the following categories:

1. Absolute beginners

2. Novices (as defined by the ACTFL Proficiency Guidelines)

3. Students with three years of Spanish, using the *¡Viva el español!* Learning Systems

4. Students with some prior knowledge of Spanish from academic or real-life experience.

The Placement Test is designed to measure the language proficiency of students in groups 2, 3, and 4, giving you an accurate evaluation of each individual's current level of competence in Spanish. Since the instructional materials in the textbooks have been designed to accommodate all of the student groups listed above, the Placement Test makes no pass/fail distinctions. The test results, however, will provide scores that will enable you to compare your students' abilities and determine your teaching strategies. The Placement Test consists of a series of short subtests for evaluating your students' language skills (listening, speaking, reading, and writing) and their mastery of the elements of language (pronunciation, grammatical structure, and vocabulary). (For your information, the descriptions of proficiency for speaking, listening, reading, and writing at the Novice and Intermediate levels can be found in the *Resource Section* of the *Annotated Teacher's Edition*.)

Unit Tests

Besides the Placement Test, there are 14–17 Unit Tests in each package, including 10–12 individual unit tests, 2–3 review tests, a mid-year test, and an end-of-year test. The Unit Tests fully cover the skills and elements taught in the textbook and accurately reflect the content of the program. While the main purpose of the Unit Tests is to help you evaluate your students' progress in mastering the textbook materials, the tests can also serve as effective review activities when you return them and discuss them with your classes. The key goal of the testing program is to teach communication in context—not as an intellectual exercise nor as a reward or punishment. In a sense, the tests become another instructional tool in helping your students develop and refine their skills.

Conducting the Tests

Conducting classroom tests can resemble a balancing act in which you strive to preserve a nonthreatening atmosphere while you maintain students' enthusiasm for learning Spanish. The following key features of the Testing Program will help you achieve this goal:

- The familiar format of the Achievement Tests will build your students' confidence because students will recognize item types and pictures from their textbooks.

- The open, uncluttered appearance of the test pages, with a limited number of test items on each, enhances readability. Your students will feel a sense of accomplishment as they complete the pages in relatively short periods of time.

• The fact that the tests are not speed tests lessens student stress. Students have no need to "beat the clock" to finish a particular section.

In keeping with the concept of promoting mastery for all students, tests are not excessively "hard," but they do contain items at various levels of difficulty so that all students will be challenged. Suggested time limits for the tests are generous (20–30 minutes) because the tests are essentially power tests, rather than speed tests. As power tests, they generally contain fewer, relatively challenging items and allow students sufficient time to complete the entire test—as opposed to speed tests, which usually feature a large number of relatively easy items but do not allow students time to finish. The technique of having students exchange test papers and score them immediately in class is recommended. By reviewing tests right after taking them, students receive immediate feedback on their errors and have a chance to master materials not yet learned. The *¡Viva el español!* textbook series tests are designed for easy correction, and they feature useful, authentic sentences suitable for oral exercises.

Test-Item Types

The *¡Viva el español!* Testing Program features an imaginative variety of test item types, including recall and recognition items. Your students will be neither surprised nor confused by unfamiliar item formats because the testing program employs the same general concepts and item types as those found in the textbook and workbook. The tests will enable you to quantify objectively your students' language skills and levels of linguistic competence, using a variety of written and oral item types that include, among others, fill-ins (letter, word, phrase, sentence); cloze items; multiple choice; true or false; matching; dictations; placing elements in logical order, or sequencing; rejoinders; naming objects; and circling words, phrases, and drawings.

Item formats used with the audio Test Cassette are largely multiple choice, true or false, and dictations, the latter progressively sequenced from letter (in the optional Part D of Section 3) to word to phrase to complete sentence fill-ins. These items assess recognition of sounds, as well as students' ability to understand words, phrases, brief sentences, and segments of conversations.

Each test section in the unit and review tests is classified according to degree of difficulty, using the following symbols:

- ○ Lowest level of difficulty
- ◐ Average level of difficulty
- ● Highest level of difficulty

The symbols indicating degree of difficulty of the test parts are found only in the Answer Key; thus, students are generally not aware that they are working with items at a specific level of difficulty. The optional, starred extra-credit items always represent the highest level of difficulty and are designed to challenge your most advanced students.

Test Content

Each test consists of three sections:

- **Section 1** is made up of lexical items based on all the active vocabulary students learn in the *¡Hablemos!* and *¿Cómo lo dices?* sections of a regular unit. These lexical items are tested in context, without resorting to English translations.

- **Section 2** consists of structural items covering all of the grammar taught in the *¿Cómo lo dices?* sections in each regular unit of the student textbook. Items are presented in meaningful contexts that will appeal to the students' imagination, sense of humor, and interests.

- **Section 3** contains listening comprehension items, made up of Parts A, B, C, and D, as follows:

  A. Listening comprehension. Students hear a brief conversation followed by five multiple-choice or true / false items, measuring students' understanding of these spoken materials.
  B. Dictation *(Dictado)*. Students listen to Spanish sentences, each repeated twice, and write the missing words and sentences.
  C. Part C, the extra-credit section, consists of five complete sentences, and features an occasional word beyond the lexicon presented in the text. This is done purposely, to give students the chance to discover how—especially with a "phonetic" language like Spanish—spelling can be deduced from sound.
  D. Sound-symbol relationships. In this optional section, students hear words and either write missing vowels or consonants or identify simple stress and intonation patterns.

For every test, Part A, Part B, and Part D are recorded on the audio Test Cassette by native speakers of Spanish. Part C has been designed to be administered by the teacher or an assistant, thus providing the students additional experience in comprehending a variety of speakers.

Placement and End-of-Year Tests

The Placement Test and the End-of-Year Test are purposely similar in form and content. In fact, section by section and item by item, these two tests are analogous with regard to form, content, and level of difficulty. This means that Placement Test scores will have real meaning in determining with precision your students' ability levels relative to the course objectives. The only deviation from this analogous structuring is the teacher-administered Speaking Section, which is found at the end of the Placement Test but not included in the End-of-Year Test. Because of the enormous amount of classroom time required to administer objective, one-on-one speaking tests, the most practical method for measuring your students' speaking ability is on an informal day-by-day basis. However, to guide you in assessing students' speaking skills at the beginning of your academic year, a brief Speaking Section has been included to supplement the other Placement Test results. In this *Testing Program* book, the Speaking Section may be found in the "Oral Test Tapescript and Guide" (see page T-25).

Administering and Scoring the Tests

Administering the Tests

The Testing Program components (blackline master book and audio Test Cassette) contain all the materials you will need for administering the tests. The only exception is the Speaking Section at the end of the Placement Test (see "Oral Test Tapescript and Guide") for which you may need classroom items and other visual aids.

Each test part includes simple written directions to the students and one or two model test items (with occasional exceptions).

For Sections 1 and 2, it is recommended that you read the instructions aloud and complete the model test item or items with the students. This will ensure that students understand clearly what they are to do and gain confidence that this item is a familiar type. By reading the directions and doing the model together, you will guarantee three factors that significantly contribute to a test's validity: clear directions, specification of the material tested, and familiarity with the test-taking technique.

Scoring the Tests

The *¡Viva el español!* Testing Program permits you to analyze test scores accurately and to give your students sufficient feedback in the form of meaningful numerical grades and positive learning reinforcement. The scores are not designed to be punitive; rather, they serve as markers for past achievement and as points of reference for further improvement. All tests allow for a separate oral achievement subscore. The Placement Test Answer Key includes guidelines for interpreting student scores to determine level of proficiency.

A Student Progress Chart is provided in the Testing Program blackline master book. On this chart, you can record your students' test scores, your informal assessment comments, and notes on individuals' strengths, as well as specific language skills that need improvement.

Because all test items are objective, the tests can be corrected quickly and easily by teachers, aides, or the students themselves. Almost all test items count one point each and can be scored on a simple all-or-nothing basis. Exceptions to this scoring are the dictation items in Parts B and C of the Oral sections of all tests. A suggested procedure for scoring these items follows:

Part B: single-word fill-ins (one point per word)

- 0.5 point off for each word that is misspelled, but recognizable

- 1 point off for each word left blank or not recognizable

Part B: complete-sentence fill-ins (two points per sentence)

- 0.5 point off for each word misspelled or left blank

- 0.5 point off for "small" errors (capitalization, punctuation) to a maximum of 1 point off per sentence for this type of error, no matter how many

- 2 points off is the maximum to be deducted from any sentence, no matter how many errors.

Part C: complete-sentence fill-ins (one extra-credit point per sentence)

Note: Score these sentences exactly like the complete-sentence fill-ins in Part B; however, because the items in Part C have a lesser point value, divide the total score for this part by two.

Your final step in the scoring process will be to convert your students' raw scores to numerical or letter grades. As scores accumulate on the Student Progress Charts and the Composite Score Chart, you can convert them at any point using the mathematics required to match them to your institution's grading system.

TEST SPECIFICATIONS

On the following pages are charts of the specifications for Sections 1, 2, and 3 of the tests.

Section 1*

Test	Words Tested	Functions	Skills	Item Types	Points
Placement	viento, cinco y cuarto, octubre, hoy, ochenta, biblioteca, cuarenta y dos, difícil, blanco, mesa, abuelos, clase, globo, hambre, divertido	functions in Unidad 1 through Unidad 10	reading, writing	matching, completion	15
Unidad 1	lápiz, hoja de papel, libro, reloj, cuaderno, mesa, pupitre, bandera, bolígrafo, ventana, mapa, borrador, tiza, regla, globo	naming classroom objects and people	reading, writing	matching, labeling	15
Unidad 2	cuadrado, círculo, triángulo, rectángulo, perro, loro, pez, mariposa, conejo, canario, amarillo, flamenco, rosado, ratón, blanco	naming colors, animals, and basic shapes	reading, writing	matching, labeling, sentence completion	15
Unidad 3	lunes, martes, miércoles, jueves, viernes, sábado, domingo, casa, cine, clase, escuela, semana, día, fin de semana, hoy	naming days of the week, telling about going places	reading, writing	matching, sentence completion, true or false	15

*Vocabulary tested is limited to the activity vocabulary that is listed in the Scope and Sequence Chart of the *Annotated Teacher's Edition* of the textbook. This is the vocabulary presented in the *¡Hablemos!* and *¿Cómo lo dices?* sections of the regular units of the textbook.

Section 1 (continued)

Test	Words Tested	Functions	Skills	Item Types	Points
Repaso: Unidades 1–3	bolígrafo, cine, cuadrado, negro, pequeño, flamenco, tiza, globo, canario, hombre	review of functions in Unidad 1 through Unidad 3	reading, writing	matching, labeling	10
Unidad 4	clase de computadoras, clase de música, clase de arte, biblioteca, gimnasio, pintar, practicar los deportes, cantar, estudiar, usar la computadora	telling about school classes and activities	reading, writing	matching, sentence completion	15
Unidad 5	invierno, verano, otoño, primavera, hace mal tiempo (frío, viento, fresco, sol), está nublado (nevando, lloviendo)	naming seasons and describing the weather	reading, writing	matching, completion, multiple choice	15
Unidad 6	enero, febrero, marzo, abril, mayo, junio, julio, agosto, septiembre, octubre, noviembre, diciembre, bailar, caminar, nadar, patinar	identifying months of the year and related activities	reading, writing	matching, sentence completion	15
Repaso: Unidades 4–6	invierno, arte, computadoras, biblioteca, casa, cantar, sol, lloviendo, bailar, patinar	review of functions in Unidad 4 through Unidad 6	reading, writing	matching-completion, sentence completion	10
Mid-Year	grande, oso, cincuenta y tres, pared, hombre, cine, casa, fin de semana, arte, pintar, verano, sol, nublado, nadar, agosto	review of functions in Unidad 1 through Unidad 6	reading, writing	matching, matching-completion, sentence completion	15

Section 1 (continued)

Test	Words Tested	Functions	Skills	Item Types	Points
Unidad 7	sueño, frío, hambre, calor, prisa, Tengo dolor (miedo, la gripe, ochenta años, razón), ¿Cuántos años tienes?, *expression of own age*	telling about self, using personal expressions	reading, writing	matching-completion, sentence completion, writing sentences	15
Unidad 8	el mediodía, la medianoche, la puesta del sol, un cuarto de hora, una media hora, una hora, en punto, la tarde, la noche, adónde, cuál, cuándo, cuántos, qué, quién	identifying lengths of time and times of day, asking questions	reading, writing	matching-completion, labeling, sentence completion	15
Unidad 9	ciencias, geografía, matemáticas, español, inglés, ciencias sociales, salud, Es aburrido (difícil, fácil, terrible, fantástico, importante, interesante), ¿Por qué?	naming school subjects, describing feelings	reading, writing	matching, writing sentences	15
Unidad 10	abuelo, abuela, bisabuela, hermano, mamá, papá, primo, prima, tío, tía, abuelos, papás, tíos, hermanos, primos	identifying and naming family members	reading, writing	matching-completion, sentence completion	15
End-of-Year	nevando, día, febrero, calor, tres y media, bandera, estudiar, fácil, rosado, abuelos, gimnasio, hambre, cuarto, treinta, setenta	review of functions in Unidad 1 through Unidad 10	reading, writing	matching, completion	15

Section 2

Test	Structures Tested	Functions	Skills	Item Types	Points
Placement	structures in Unidad 1 through Unidad 10	functions in Unidad 1 through Unidad 10	reading, writing	rewriting sentences, sentence completion	20
Unidad 1	definite articles; singular/ plural of nouns	identifying and naming classroom objects	reading, writing	sentence completion, multiple-choice	20 ★ 5
Unidad 2	adjectives: gender and number, indefinite articles	identifying and naming animals; describing animals and objects	reading, writing	sentence completion, matching	20 ★ 5
Unidad 3	singular, present tense of *ir*; definite article with days of the week; *a* + definite articles	telling about going places, using the days of the week	reading, writing	sentence completion, slash sentence	20 ★ 5
Repaso: Unidades 1–3	review of structures in Unidad 1 through Unidad 3	review of functions in Unidad 1 through Unidad 3	reading, writing	sentence completion	15
Unidad 4	*ir a* + infinitive (singular); singular present tense of regular *-ar* verbs	telling about school-related activities; talking about future actions	reading, writing	sentence completion, question and answer	20 ★ 5
Unidad 5	present-tense singular forms of *gustar*; use of adjectives as nouns; negative construction	discussing likes and dislikes	reading, writing	sentence completion, sentence editing, sentence composition	20 ★ 5

★ = extra credit

Section 2 (continued)

Test	Structures Tested	Functions	Skills	Item Types	Points
Unidad 6	singular subject pronouns; frequency expressions	telling about people's activities	reading, writing	multiple-choice, sentence completion	20 ★ 5
Repaso: Unidades 4–6	review of structures in Unidad 4 through Unidad 6	review of functions in Unidad 4 through Unidad 6	reading, writing	multiple-choice, sentence completion, matching-completion	15
Mid-Year	review of structures in Unidad 1 through Unidad 6	review of functions in Unidad 1 through Unidad 6	reading, writing	rewriting sentences, sentence completion, matching-completion	20
Unidad 7	*tú* and *usted*; present-tense singular of *tener*	addressing others familiarly or formally; telling about feelings	reading, writing	sentence completion, contextual matching	20 ★ 5
Unidad 8	interrogative words; telling time	asking questions; telling time	reading, writing	matching-completion, multiple-choice, writing sentences, question and answer	20 ★ 5
Unidad 9	present-tense third-person plural form of *gustar*; singular indirect object pronouns; present-tense singular forms of regular -*er* and -*ir* verbs	asking and telling about likes and dislikes; asking and telling about everyday activities	reading, writing	sentence completion	20 ★ 5

Section 2 (continued)

Test	Structures Tested	Functions	Skills	Item Types	Points
Unidad 10	singular and plural of possessive adjectives: *mi, tu, su*; diminutive endings *-ito, -itos, -ita, -itas*	expressing ownership; expressing size or endearment	reading, writing	sentence completion	20 ★ 5
End-of-Year	review of structures in Unidad 1 through Unidad 10	review of functions in Unidad 1 through Unidad 10	reading, writing	completion, rewriting sentences	20

Section 3

Test	Skills	Conversation Source	Auditory Item Types	Sounds Tested**	Points
Placement	listening, writing, speaking	new*	multiple-choice, dictation (word, sentence), question / answer (Speaking Test)	vowel and consonant sounds in Unidad 1 through Unidad 10	25 10 optional
Unidad 1	listening, writing	Resource and Activity Book Master 107	true or false, dictation (word, sentence)	*a*	15 ★ 5 10 optional
Unidad 2	listening, writing	Resource and Activity Book Master 108	true or false, dictation (word, sentence)	*a, o*	15 ★ 5 10 optional
Unidad 3	listening, writing	Resource and Activity Book Master 109	true or false, dictation (word, sentence)	*e, u*	15 ★ 5 10 optional
Repaso: Unidades 1–3	listening, writing	new	true or false, dictation (word, sentence)	*a, e, o, u*	15 10 optional
Unidad 4	listening, writing	Resource and Activity Book Master 110	multiple-choice, dictation (word, sentence)	*i*	15 ★ 5 10 optional
Unidad 5	listening, writing	Resource and Activity Book Master 111	multiple-choice, dictation (word, sentence)	*a, e, i, o, u*	15 ★ 5 10 optional

*   For the text of new conversations, see pages T-23–T-53, "Oral Test Tapescript and Guide."
** Listening discrimination test parts appearing at the end of Section 3 are optional.
★ = extra credit

Section 3 (continued)

Test	Skills	Conversation Source	Auditory Item Types	Sounds Tested**	Points
Unidad 6	listening, writing	Resource and Activity Book Master 112	true or false, dictation (word, sentence)	*a, e*	15 ★ 5 10 optional
Repaso: Unidades 4–6	listening, writing	new	true or false, dictation (word, sentence)	*a, e, i, o, u*	15 10 optional
Mid-Year	listening, writing	new	multiple-choice, dictation (word, sentence)	*a, e, i, o, u*	15 10 optional
Unidad 7	listening, writing	Resource and Activity Book Master 113	true or false, dictation (word, sentence)	*e, i*	15 ★ 5 10 optional
Unidad 8	listening, writing	Resource and Activity Book Master 114	true or false, dictation (word, sentence)	*o, u*	15 ★ 5 10 optional
Unidad 9	listening, writing	Resource and Activity Book Master 115	true or false, dictation (word, sentence)	*d*	15 ★ 5 10 optional
Unidad 10	listening, writing	Resource and Activity Book Master 116	true or false, dictation (word, sentence)	*p, t*	15 ★ 5 10 optional
End-of-Year	listening, writing	new	multiple-choice, dictation (word, sentence)	review of vowel and consonant sounds in Unidad 1 through Unidad 10	15 10 optional

ORAL TEST TAPESCRIPT & GUIDE

In this section you will find the scripts for the oral sections of all the tests in the testing program. The scripts will help you preview the parts that are recorded on the audio Test Cassette and prepare for the teacher-administered parts of the oral sections. The following symbol indicates that the material has been recorded on the Test Cassette:

Conducting the Oral Section (Section 3)

The objective of a listening-comprehension assessment tool is to measure understanding of the language as it is spoken at a normal, natural pace by native speakers. It is recommended that you monitor your students as they listen to the Test Cassette and, if necessary, pause the tape to allow more time to write or rewind the tape and play a part again (for example, the conversation in Part A of each Oral Section [Section 3]).

Most of the material in Section 3 of each test should be familiar to students if you have presented each section of the regular units in the textbook. Therefore, your decision to pause or replay a specific part should be based on your students' abilities, their familiarity with the unit sections, and their exposure to the language and grammar of a unit as spoken by native speakers (i.e., the sections recorded on the Lesson and Exercise cassettes).

When you present the teacher-administered part of Section 3, it is recommended that you speak clearly, pleasantly, and at a natural, comfortable pace. You may wish to conduct practice dictations prior to the testing situation to determine an appropriate pace: a pace that is too slow may result in students becoming bored and easily distracted; a pace that is too fast may result in frustration and a negative attitude toward the testing experience. Because the tests are power tests and not speed tests, the objective is to obtain an accurate measure of students' ability to comprehend the spoken language while maintaining their enthusiasm for learning Spanish as a second language.

PLACEMENT TEST [Test masters 7–8]*

A. First listen to the conversation between Julia and Carlos. Then you will hear five multiple-choice statements about their conversation. You will hear each statement twice. Circle the letter of the word or phrase that best completes each statement.

JULIA: Carlos, ¿Te gusta la clase de español?
CARLOS: Sí, Julia, y me gustan las matemáticas. Pero la clase de inglés es terrible.
JULIA: ¿Terrible?
CARLOS: Sí, porque no me gusta mi pupitre. Es muy pequeño.
JULIA: ¿El pupitre es pequeño o tú eres grande?
CARLOS: ¡Muy divertida! No, el pupitre es pequeño. ¿Cómo son los pupitres en tu salón de clase?
JULIA: Mi salón de clase es el número 15. No tiene pupitres. Tiene mesas grandes.
CARLOS: ¡Ah, me gusta mucho el salón número 15. ¡Es un salón fantástico!

[Each multiple-choice statement is given twice on the Test Cassette.]

1. A Carlos le gusta...
  a. el pupitre.
  b. la clase de español.
  c. la clase de historia.

2. El pupitre de Carlos es...
  a. grande.
  b. importante.
  c. pequeño.

3. La clase de inglés de Carlos es...
  a. terrible.
  b. fácil.
  c. fantástico.

4. El salón número 15 no tiene...
  a. mesas.
  b. pupitres.
  c. alumnos.

5. A Carlos le gusta mucho...
  a. el inglés.
  b. su pupitre.
  c. el salón número 15.

B. Dictado. Listen carefully to these sentences. You will hear each sentence twice. Write the missing words on the answer blanks.

[Each sentence is given twice on the Test Cassette.]

1. El ratón es un animal pequeño.
2. No me gustan los ratones.
3. Yo tengo dos gatos.
4. El gato negro tiene ojos amarillos.
5. El gato gris tiene ojos azules.

---

*Notes regarding the tests are presented in this section in brackets and italic letters. They are not recorded on the Test Cassette.

C. Speaking

[The Speaking Section of the Placement Test contains ten questions that count one point each. Credit should be given for the accuracy, completeness, and appropriateness of each answer. Students should be encouraged to answer each question as completely as they can, but should not be penalized for failure to use complete sentences. Although natural, conversational responses are the goal, a one-word response should be given full credit if it is correct.

Materials Needed: a number card between 10 and 100 (Teacher's Resource and Activity Book); an animal vocabulary card, such as a dog, bird, tiger, or cat (Teacher's Resource and Activity Book); a classroom object, such as a pen, chalk eraser, book, or notebook; a sheet of colored construction paper in red, yellow, blue, or green; a clock or watch; a calendar in Spanish (optional).]

1. ¿Cómo estás?
2. ¿Cómo te llamas?
3. ¿Qué número es? *[Hold up a number card between 10 and 100.]*
4. ¿Qué es esto? *[Point to or hold up a classroom object.]*
5. ¿Qué es esto? *[Hold up an animal vocabulary card.]*
6. ¿De qué color es? *[Hold up a sheet of colored construction paper.]*
7. ¿Qué hora es? *[Point to a clock or watch.]*
8. ¿Qué día es hoy? *[Optional: Point to a calendar in Spanish.]*
9. ¿Qué tiempo hace hoy?
10. ¿Cuántos años tienes?

D. Listen carefully to these words. You will hear each word twice. Complete each word by writing a vowel or consonant letter on the answer blank. The first two have been done for you. (This test part is optional. Point values should not be applied to students' scores.)

1. hace, hace
2. gato, gato
3. nadar, nadar
4. suerte, suerte
5. noche, noche
6. inglés, inglés
7. oreja, oreja
8. nunca, nunca
9. aburrido, aburrido
10. llueve, llueve
11. año, año
12. gusta, gusta

A. Listen to the conversation between Carlos and Olga. Then you will hear five statements about their conversation. You will hear each statement twice. Circle **CIERTO** if the statement is true. Circle **FALSO** if it is false.

OLGA:	¡Hola, Carlos! ¿Cómo estás?
CARLOS:	Muy bien, Olga. ¿Y tú?
OLGA:	Muy bien. ¿Qué es esto? ¿Es un bolígrafo?
CARLOS:	No, Olga, no es un bolígrafo. Es un lápiz.
OLGA:	Carlos, ¿qué es...?
CARLOS:	¡Hasta luego, Olga! ¡Qué aburrida!

¿Cierto o falso?

[Each statement is given twice on the Test Cassette.]

1. Carlos es el muchacho.
2. La muchacha se llama Olga.
3. Carlos no está muy bien.
4. Olga es la profesora de Carlos.
5. Hay un lápiz.

 B. Dictado. Listen carefully to these sentences and phrases. You will hear each one twice. Write the missing word on the answer blank. The first one has been done for you.

[Each sentence and phrase is given twice on the Test Cassette.]

1. ¿Qué es esto?
2. el salón de clase
3. Se llama David.
4. el señor Rodríguez
5. ¿Está bien Olga?
6. Son los cuadernos.
7. Es el globo.
8. ¿Hay dos profesores?
9. ¿Cuántos hay?
10. El muchacho está muy bien.
11. Me llamo Carlos.

C. Now try writing these sentences for extra credit. You will hear each sentence twice.

[Read each of the following sentences twice in a loud, clear, pleasant voice.]

1. La muchacha se llama Juana.
2. Hay seis bolígrafos en la mesa.

3. La pizarra está en el salón de clase.

4. Hay un mapa en la pared.

5. Hay tres libros, profesora.

D. You will hear a number and a word. If the word contains an **a** sound, circle the number. If the word does not have an **a** sound, do not circle the number. The first two have been done for you. (This test part is optional. Point values should not be applied to students' scores.)

(**1.**) adiós

2. pronto

3. mesa

4. bueno

5. nada

6. computadora

7. perro

8. deportes

9. bolígrafo

10. boxeo

11. cine

12. estás

A. Listen to the conversation between Ana and Marcos. Then you will hear five statements about their conversation. You will hear each statement twice. Circle **CIERTO** if the statement is true. Circle **FALSO** if it is false.

ANA:	Por favor, Marcos, pásame el círculo rojo.
MARCOS:	¿El círculo grande?
ANA:	No, Marcos, el círculo pequeño. Gracias. Marcos, pásame un triángulo azul.
MARCOS:	¿El triángulo verde?
ANA:	No, Marcos, el triángulo azul. Gracias. Ahora, pásame un rectángulo amarillo.
MARCOS:	¿Un rectángulo grande?
ANA:	No, Marcos, un rectángulo pequeño. Muchas gracias. Por favor, Marcos, pásame…
MARCOS:	¡Adiós, Ana! ¡Hasta luego!
ANA:	¡Marcos!

¿Cierto o falso?

[Each statement is given twice on the Test Cassette.]
1. La muchacha se llama Marcos.
2. El círculo es rojo.
3. El rectángulo es amarillo.
4. Marcos es el alumno de Ana.
5. Hay un rectángulo pequeño.

B. Dictado. Listen to these sentences and write the missing words. You will hear each sentence twice.

[Each sentence is given twice on the Test Cassette.]
1. El círculo es pequeño.
2. El rectángulo es grande.
3. ¡Hasta luego!
4. El triángulo es azul.
5. Sí, profesora. ¡Muchas gracias!

C. Now try writing these sentences for extra credit. You will hear each sentence twice.

[Read each of the following sentences twice.]
1. ¿Cómo es el conejo?
2. El conejo es pequeño.
3. ¿Cuál es tu animal favorito?
4. Mi animal favorito es el flamenco.
5. ¿De qué color es?

D. Listen carefully to these twelve words. You will hear each word twice. Complete each word by writing **a** or **o** on the answer blank. The first two have been done for you. (This test part is optional. Point values should not be applied to students' scores.)

1. libros, libros
2. clase, clase
3. amarilla, amarilla
4. señor, señor

5. ratones, ratones
6. España, España
7. Bolivia, Bolivia
8. nuestra, nuestra

9. votar, votar
10. vamos, vamos
11. claro, claro
12. gato, gato

UNIDAD 3: UNIT TEST *[Test masters 30–31]*

A. Listen to the conversation between Carmen and Isidro. Then you will hear five statements about their conversation. You will hear each statement twice. Circle **CIERTO** if the statement is true. Circle **FALSO** if it is false.

CARMEN:	¡Hola, Isidro!
ISIDRO:	¿Qué tal, Carmen?
CARMEN:	Muy bien, gracias. ¿Adónde vas esta semana?
ISIDRO:	El lunes y el martes voy a la escuela. Voy con dos cuadernos y tres libros. El miércoles y el jueves voy a la escuela con seis libros.
CARMEN:	¿Y el viernes?
ISIDRO:	Hoy voy a la escuela con el lápiz amarillo, tres libros y un cuaderno.
CARMEN:	Isidro, ¡hoy es sábado! ¡No vas a la escuela hoy!

¿Cierto o falso?

[Each statement is given twice on the Test Cassette.]
1. El muchacho se llama Isidro.
2. Isidro va al cine.
3. Esta semana, Isidro va a la escuela.
4. El lápiz es amarillo.
5. Hoy es domingo.

B. Dictado. Listen carefully to these sentences. You will hear each sentence twice. Write the missing words on the answer blanks.

[Each sentence is given twice on the Test Cassette.]
1. ¿Qué día es el dos?
2. El dos es jueves.
3. ¿Vas a la escuela hoy?
4. No, no voy a la escuela hoy.
5. Ella va a la casa de Carlos.

C. Now try writing these sentences for extra credit. You will hear each sentence twice.

[Read each of the following sentences twice.]
1. ¿Quién es esta muchacha?
2. No hay calendario.
3. ¿Adónde va Paco?
4. Carmen va a casa.
5. Esta semana no hay clase.

D. Listen carefully to these twelve words. You will hear each word twice. Complete each word by writing **e** or **u** on the answer blank. The first two have been done for you. (This test part is optional. Point values should not be applied to students' scores.)

1. Ernesto, Ernesto
2. una, una
3. lunes, lunes
4. martes, martes

5. cine, cine
6. jueves, jueves
7. luna, luna
8. azul, azul

9. uva, uva
10. semana, semana
11. esta, esta
12. ¿adónde?, ¿adónde?

REPASO: UNIDADES 1-3 ACHIEVEMENT REVIEW TEST
[Test masters 35–36]

A. Listen to the conversation between Paula and Miguel. Then you will hear five statements about their conversation. You will hear each statement twice. Circle **CIERTO** if the statement is true. Circle **FALSO** if it is false.

PAULA:	¡Hola, Miguel! ¿Cómo estás?
MIGUEL:	¡Buenas tardes, Paula! Estoy así, así. ¿Y tú?
PAULA:	Estoy muy bien.
MIGUEL:	¿Qué son estos?
PAULA:	Son unos peces pequeños. El pez es mi animal favorito.
MIGUEL:	¿Cuántos peces hay?
PAULA:	Hay cuatro peces. Miguel, ¿cuál es tu animal favorito?
MIGUEL:	Es el perro.
PAULA:	¿De qué color es tu perro favorito?
MIGUEL:	Es blanco, negro y marrón.
PAULA:	¡Adiós, Miguel! Voy a casa. Hasta el lunes.
MIGUEL:	Voy al cine ahora. ¡Nos vemos pronto!

¿Cierto o falso?

[Each statement is given twice on the Test Cassette.]
1. Miguel está así, así.
2. El pez es el animal favorito de Paula.
3. Hay cinco peces.
4. El animal favorito de Miguel es el perro.
5. Miguel va a casa.

B. Dictado. Listen to these sentences and write the missing words. You will hear each sentence twice.

[Each sentence is given twice on the Test Cassette.]
1. La muchacha se llama Carmen.
2. El triángulo es pequeño.
3. El día quince es viernes.
4. ¿Quién va a casa?
5. Hay un mapa en la mesa.

C. Listen carefully to these words. You will hear each word twice. Complete each word by writing **a, e, o,** or **u** on the answer blank. The first one has been done for you. (This test part is optional. Point values should not be applied to students' scores.)

1. gato, gato
2. pez, pez
3. oscuro, oscuro
4. oso, oso

5. ¿adónde?, ¿adónde?
6. voy, voy
7. pluma, pluma
8. ventana, ventana

9. silla, silla
10. bolígrafo, bolígrafo
11. cine, cine

UNIDAD 4: UNIT TEST [Test masters 43–44]

A. Listen to the conversation between Teresa and Pablo. Then you will hear five multiple-choice statements about their conversation. You will hear each statement twice. Circle the letter of the phrase that best completes each statement.

TERESA: ¿Adónde vas, Pablo?

PABLO: Voy a las clases, Teresa.

TERESA: ¿Qué vas a hacer en la clase de computadoras?

PABLO: Voy a usar la computadora.

TERESA: ¿Vas a cantar en la clase de música?

PABLO: Sí, canto muy bien. ¿Adónde vas tú?

TERESA: Voy al gimnasio.

PABLO: ¿Vas a practicar los deportes?

TERESA: ¡No! Voy a estudiar en el gimnasio. ¡Practico los deportes en la biblioteca!

[Each multiple-choice statement is given twice on the Test Cassette.]

1. Pablo va...

   a.   al gimnasio.

   b.   a las clases.

   c.   a la clase de español.

4. Pablo va a usar...

   a.   la biblioteca.

   b.   el gimnasio.

   c.   la computadora.

2. Pablo canta...

   a.   muy mal.

   b.   así, así.

   c.   muy bien.

5. Teresa es...

   a.   profesora.

   b.   alumna.

   c.   profesor.

3. Teresa va...

   a.   al gimnasio.

   b.   a la clase de computadoras.

   c.   a la biblioteca.

B. Dictado. Listen carefully to these sentences. You will hear each sentence twice. Write the missing words on the answer blanks.

[Each sentence is given twice on the Test Cassette.]

1. ¿Pintas muy bien?

2. ¿Cantas en la clase de música?

3. Norma usa la computadora.

4. Pablo va a estudiar.

5. Voy a ir al cine.

C. Now try writing these sentences for extra credit. You will hear each sentence twice.

[Read each of the following sentences twice.]

1. ¿Qué vas a hacer el lunes?
2. Mañana es domingo, ¿no?
3. ¿Qué hace Paula en la escuela?
4. ¡Es una muchacha pequeña!
5. Hay cuatro libros en el salón de clase.

 D. You will hear a number and a word. If the word contains an **i** sound, circle the number. If the word does not have an **i** sound, do not circle the number. The first two have been done for you. (This test part is optional. Point values should not be applied to students' scores.)

1. escuela
2. pintas
3. tiza
4. libro
5. deportes
6. usar
7. cinco
8. mira
9. Tomás
10. amarillo
11. arte
12. Isidro

UNIDAD 5: UNIT TEST [Test masters 51–52]

A. Listen to the conversation between Fernando and Daniel. Then you will hear five multiple-choice statements about their conversation. You will hear each statement twice. Circle the letter of the phrase that best completes each statement.

FERNANDO: ¿Te gusta el verano?

DANIEL: Sí. En el verano hace buen tiempo. Hace sol y hace calor.

FERNANDO: ¿Te gusta el invierno?

DANIEL: No. En el invierno hace mal tiempo. Nieva y hace frío.

FERNANDO: En la primavera está nublado y llueve. Daniel, ¿te gusta la primavera?

DANIEL: Sí, me gusta. Hace fresco en la primavera.

FERNANDO: En el otoño hace viento y… ¿Qué voy a hacer? ¡Está lloviendo!

[Each multiple-choice statement is given twice on the Test Cassette.]

1. A Daniel le gusta…
   a. el invierno.
   b. el otoño.
   c. el verano.

2. A Daniel no le gusta…
   a. el invierno.
   b. la primavera.
   c. el verano.

3. En el otoño hace…
   a. calor.
   b. viento.
   c. sol.

4. En la primavera hace…
   a. calor.
   b. fresco.
   c. frío.

5. Ahora está…
   a. lloviendo.
   b. nevando.
   c. nublado.

B. **Dictado.** Listen carefully to these sentences. You will hear each sentence twice. Write the missing words on the answer blanks.

[Each sentence is given twice on the Test Cassette.]

1. Hay una mesa larga.
2. ¿Cuántas luces azules hay?
3. A Paula le gusta cantar.
4. Hace calor en el verano.
5. Hace frío y está nevando.

C. Now try writing these sentences for extra credit. You will hear each sentence twice.

[Read each of the following sentences twice.]
1. ¿Cuáles son las estaciones?
2. ¿Qué te gusta hacer?
3. En la primavera llueve.
4. Hace muy buen tiempo hoy.
5. ¿No te gusta el invierno?

D. Listen carefully. Then complete the words by writing **a, e, i, o,** or **u.** You will hear each word twice. The first two have been done for you. (This test part is optional. Point values should not be applied to students' scores.)

1. estación, estación	5. primavera, primavera	9. nunca, nunca
2. nacer, nacer	6. lluvia, lluvia	10. fresco, fresco
3. gusta, gusta	7. hace, hace	11. estudio, estudio
4. invierno, invierno	8. oficina, oficina	12. calor, calor

A. Listen to the conversation between Ernesto and Clarita. Then you will hear five statements about their conversation. You will hear each statement twice. Circle **CIERTO** if the statement is true. Circle **FALSO** if it is false.

ERNESTO:	¡Hola, Clarita! Estoy en el Uruguay. ¡Qué calor hace!
CLARITA:	¿Calor? No, Ernesto. Hace frío. Es enero y hace frío.
ERNESTO:	¡Ja, ja, ja! Clarita, ¡estoy en Montevideo! ¡Aquí es el verano!
CLARITA:	¿El verano? Pues, ¿cuáles son los meses del invierno?
ERNESTO:	Son junio, julio y agosto.
CLARITA:	Y... ¿practicas los deportes?
ERNESTO:	Sí. Nado mucho en el océano.
CLARITA:	¡Mamá! ¡Mamá! ¡Voy al Uruguay!

¿Cierto o falso?

[Each statement is given twice on the Test Cassette.]

1. Hace calor en Uruguay.
2. En Uruguay es el invierno.
3. Ernesto practica los deportes.
4. En Uruguay, los meses de invierno son junio, julio y agosto.
5. Clarita nada mucho.

 B. Dictado. Listen and write the missing words. You will hear each sentence twice.

[Each sentence is given twice on the Test Cassette.]

1. ¿Te gusta nadar?
2. Sí, me gusta.
3. ¿Nadas mucho en mayo?
4. No. Nado en julio.
5. ¿Qué haces en octubre?

C. Now try writing these sentences for extra credit. You will hear each sentence twice.

[Read each of the following sentences twice.]

1. ¿Quién pinta?
2. Yo pinto muy bien.
3. ¿Pinta Isabel?
4. No, ella no pinta.
5. Rita pinta muy bien.

D. Listen carefully to the following twelve words. You will hear each word twice. Complete each word by writing **a** or **e** on the answer blank. The first two have been done for you. (This test part is optional. Point values should not be applied to students' scores.)

1. marzo, marzo
2. enero, enero
3. te, te
4. agosto, agosto

5. patinar, patinar
6. hace, hace
7. diciembre, diciembre
8. caminar, caminar

9. nadar, nadar
10. septiembre, septiembre
11. bailar, bailar
12. verano, verano

REPASO: UNIDADES 4-6 ACHIEVEMENT REVIEW TEST
[Test masters 65–66]

A. Listen to the conversation between Mateo and Andrea. Then you will hear five statements about their conversation. You will hear each statement twice. Circle **CIERTO** if the statement is true. Circle **FALSO** if it is false.

MATEO:	¡Muy buenos días, Andrea!
ANDREA:	¡Hola, Mateo! ¿Qué vas a hacer hoy?
MATEO:	Voy a patinar. Siempre patino los sábados.
ANDREA:	A mí no me gusta patinar. Me gusta bailar. Siempre bailo los sábados.
MATEO:	¿No practicas los deportes?
ANDREA:	Pues, sí. A veces practico los deportes. ¿Nunca bailas tú?
MATEO:	¡Nunca! No me gusta bailar. No bailo muy bien.
ANDREA:	¿No bailas? ¿Te gusta ir al cine?
MATEO:	¡Sí! Me gusta mucho. ¿A ti te gusta ir al cine?
ANDREA:	Sí, voy al cine esta noche.
MATEO:	Yo también. Hasta más tarde.
ANDREA:	¡Hasta luego!

¿Cierto o falso?

[Each statement is given twice on the Test Cassette.]
1. Mateo va a patinar.
2. A Andrea le gusta patinar.
3. Mateo no baila bien.
4. A Mateo le gusta ir al cine.
5. Andrea no va al cine.

B. Dictado. Listen carefully to these sentences. You will hear each sentence twice. Write the missing words on the answer blanks.

[Each sentence is given twice on the Test Cassette.]
1. A Norma le gusta cantar.
2. Ella canta muy bien en la clase de música.
3. Me gusta usar la computadora.
4. Ahora voy a la clase de arte.
5. Me gusta pintar.

C. Listen carefully to these words. You will hear each word twice. Complete each word by writing **a, e, i, o,** or **u** on the answer blank. The first two have been done for you. (This test part is optional. Point values should not be applied to students' scores.)

1. cine, cine
2. pintar, pintar
3. deportes, deportes
4. gusta, gusta

5. sol, sol
6. patinar, patinar
7. casa, casa
8. mucho, mucho

9. arte, arte
10. diciembre, diciembre
11. invierno, invierno
12. estudio, estudio

MID-YEAR TEST [Test masters 73–74]

A. Listen to the conversation between Ernesto and Clarita. Then you will hear five multiple-choice statements about the conversation. You will hear each statement twice. Circle the letter of the word or phrase that best completes each statement.

ERNESTO: ¡Huy! Hace mucho frío.

CLARITA: Sí, Ernesto. En invierno hace mal tiempo.

ERNESTO: ¡Es terrible! ¿Cómo es el verano?

CLARITA: En verano hace mucho calor.

ERNESTO: Me gusta el calor. En verano voy a nadar.

CLARITA: Yo no voy a nadar en verano. Voy a estudiar.

ERNESTO: ¿Vas a estudiar, Clarita? Mm... ¿Qué vas a estudiar?

CLARITA: Voy a estudiar computadoras.

ERNESTO: ¿Cómo es la clase de computadoras?

CLARITA: Muy larga, Ernesto, muy, muy larga.

[Each multiple-choice statement is given twice on the Test Cassette.]

1. Ahora hace mucho...
   a. calor.
   b. frío.
   c. sol.

2. A Ernesto no le gusta...
   a. el invierno.
   b. el verano.
   c. el otoño.

3. A Ernesto le gusta...
   a. el frío.
   b. el viento.
   c. el calor.

4. En verano, Clarita va a...
   a. estudiar.
   b. nadar.
   c. bailar.

5. La clase de computadoras es muy...
   a. extraña.
   b. grande.
   c. larga.

B. Dictado. Listen carefully to these sentences. You will hear each sentence twice. Write the missing words on the answer blanks.

[Each sentence is given twice on the Test Cassette.]

1. Hay cuatro libros en la mesa.
2. ¿Dónde está la alumna?
3. Hace muy buen tiempo.
4. Ella nada en el verano.
5. ¿No va a la escuela hoy?

C. Listen carefully to these words. You will hear each word twice. Complete each word by writing **a, e, i, o,** or **u** on the answer blank. The first two have been done for you. (This test part is optional. Point values should not be applied to students' scores.)

1. agosto, agosto
2. invierno, invierno
3. hace, hace
4. oscuro, oscuro

5. largo, largo
6. domingo, domingo
7. música, música
8. azul, azul

9. esta, esta
10. gimnasio, gimnasio
11. mayo, mayo
12. pluma, pluma

A. Listen to this conversation between Dora, Adela, and Arturo. Then you will hear five statements about their conversation. You will hear each statement twice. Circle **CIERTO** if the statement is true. Circle **FALSO** if it is false.

DORA:	¡Hola! ¿Cómo estás, Arturo? ¡Qué gusto en verte!
ARTURO:	Estoy muy bien, gracias. ¿Qué tal, Adela?
ADELA:	Estoy así, así. Tengo mucha sed.
ARTURO:	¿Y tú, Dora?
DORA:	Yo tengo un poco de hambre.
ADELA:	Arturo, siéntate, por favor.
ARTURO:	No, gracias. Tengo mucha prisa. Adiós, muchachas.
ADELA:	Hasta pronto, Arturo.
DORA:	¿Qué lástima! Hoy no tengo suerte.

¿Cierto o falso?

[Each statement is given twice on the Test Cassette.]
1. Arturo está muy bien.
2. Adela tiene mucha sed.
3. Dora tiene mucha hambre.
4. Arturo tiene mucha prisa.
5. Dora tiene suerte.

B. Dictado. Listen, and then write the missing words. You will hear each sentence twice.

[Each sentence is given twice on the Test Cassette.]
1. ¿Cuántos años tiene la señorita Cortéz?
2. ¿Alicia? Tiene quince años.
3. ¿Le gusta la escuela?
4. Sí, le gusta mucho estudiar.
5. Ella tiene muchos libros.

C. Now try writing these sentences for extra credit. You will hear each sentence twice.

[Read each of the following sentences twice.]
1. ¿Tienes hambre?
2. No, no tengo hambre.
3. ¿Tienes calor?
4. Sí, tengo mucho calor.
5. ¡Muchacha, tú tienes la gripe!

D. Listen carefully to these twelve words. You will hear each word twice. Complete each word by writing **e** or **i** on the answer blank. The first two have been done for you. (This test part is optional. Point values should not be applied to students' scores.)

1. leche, leche
2. cinco, cinco
3. viven, viven
4. vemos, vemos

5. peso, peso
6. piso, piso
7. prisa, prisa
8. sed, sed

9. gripe, gripe
10. hervida, hervida
11. tres, tres
12. suerte, suerte

A. Listen to the conversation between Mónica, Pedro, and Pedro's mother. Then you will hear five statements about their conversation. You will hear each statement twice. Circle **CIERTO** if the statement is true. Circle **FALSO** if it is false.

MÓNICA:	Hola, Pedro. ¿A qué hora vas a la escuela el lunes?
PEDRO:	Hola, Mónica. A las ocho y media de la mañana.
MÓNICA:	¿A qué hora vas a estudiar esta tarde?
PEDRO:	¿Qué hora es?
MÓNICA:	Son las tres y cuarto. Voy a estudiar a las tres y media. ¿Vas a estudiar a las tres y media también?
PEDRO:	¡Claro que no! Nunca estudio. No me gusta estudiar.
MAMÁ:	Pedro, son las tres y veinte. ¡Esta tarde vas a estudiar dos horas!
PEDRO:	¡Ay, mamá! ¡Es el fin de semana!
MÓNICA:	¿Nunca estudias, eh? Hasta mañana, Pedro.
PEDRO:	Hasta mañana, Mónica.

¿Cierto o falso?

[Each statement is given twice on the Test Cassette.]
1. Pedro va a la escuela el lunes.
2. Mónica va a estudiar a las tres y media.
3. Pedro nunca estudia.
4. Es viernes.
5. Es el fin de semana.

B. Dictado. Listen carefully to these sentences. You will hear each sentence twice. Write the missing words on the answer blanks.

[Each sentence is given twice on the Test Cassette.]
1. José va a la escuela a las ocho de la mañana.
2. A José le gusta estudiar.
3. A las cuatro en punto, José va a casa.
4. En casa, José estudia dos horas.
5. José estudia a las nueve de la noche.

C. Now try writing these sentences for extra credit. You will hear each sentence twice.

[Read each of the following sentences twice.]
1. ¿Cuántos minutos hay en media hora?
2. Hay treinta minutos.
3. ¿Cuántos minutos hay en un cuarto de hora?
4. Hay quince minutos.
5. Muchas gracias, profesora.

D. Listen carefully to the following twelve words. You will hear each word twice. Complete each word by writing **o** or **u** on the answer blank. The first two have been done for you. (This test part is optional. Point values should not be applied to students' scores.)

1. hora, hora	5. punto, punto	9. ¿cuándo?, ¿cuándo?
2. minuto, minuto	6. sol, sol	10. ¿cómo?, ¿cómo?
3. cuarto, cuarto	7. mula, mula	11. gusta, gusta
4. una, una	8. noche, noche	12. mucho, mucho

UNIDAD 9: UNIT TEST [Test masters 97–98]

A. Listen to the conversation between Alejandro and señor López. Then you will hear five statements about their conversation. You will hear each statement twice. Circle **CIERTO** if the statement is true. Circle **FALSO** if it is false.

SR. LÓPEZ:	Alejandro, ¿qué clases te gustan?
ALEJANDRO:	Bueno, señor López, me gustan las clases de computadoras, el español y la educación física.
SR. LÓPEZ:	¿Cuál es tu clase favorita?
ALEJANDRO:	La clase de español. ¡Es fantástica!
SR. LÓPEZ:	¿Qué clase no te gusta?
ALEJANDRO:	No me gusta la clase de geografía. Es muy difícil.
SR. LÓPEZ:	¿De veras? ¿Te gustan las matemáticas?
ALEJANDRO:	¡Claro que no! Es una clase muy aburrida. ¡Es terrible! Y usted, ¿es profesor?
SR. LÓPEZ:	Sí. Soy el profesor de matemáticas.
ALEJANDRO:	¡Ay! ¡Disculpe, profesor! Hasta luego.
SR. LÓPEZ:	¡Hasta pronto, muchacho!

¿Cierto o falso?

[Each statement is given twice on the Test Cassette.]
1. A Alejandro le gusta la clase de educación física.
2. La clase favorita de Alejandro es la geografía.
3. A Alejandro no le gusta la clase de español.
4. A Alejandro no le gustan las matemáticas.
5. El señor López es profesor de matemáticas.

B. Dictado. Listen carefully and write the missing words. You will hear each sentence twice.

[Each sentence is given twice on the Test Cassette.]
1. Aprendo mucho en la escuela.
2. Los profesores son fantásticos.
3. Las clases son muy interesantes.
4. Tengo dos clases importantes.
5. Son las clases de español y de matemáticas.
6. No me gusta la clase de educación física.

C. Now try writing these phrases and sentences for extra credit. You will hear each one twice.

[Read each of the following sentences twice.]
1. ¿Por qué estudias español?
2. Porque me gusta.
3. ¿Dónde estudias?
4. En la escuela y en casa.
5. El español es muy divertido.

 D. Listen carefully to the thirteen words that follow. You will hear each word twice. If you hear the consonant **d** in a word, circle **sí.** If you do not hear the consonant **d**, circle **no.** The first three have been done for you. (This test part is optional. Point values should not be applied to students' scores.)

1. día, día
2. terrible, terrible
3. usted, usted
4. dolor, dolor
5. aburrido, aburrido
6. vivo, vivo
7. difícil, difícil

8. salud, salud
9. inglés, inglés
10. educación, educación
11. hora, hora
12. verdad, verdad
13. importante, importante

UNIDAD 10: UNIT TEST [Test masters 104–105]

A. Listen to the conversation between Luisa and Eduardo. Then you will hear five statements about their conversation. You will hear each statement twice. Circle **CIERTO** if the statement is true. Circle **FALSO** if it is false.

EDUARDO: Luisa, ¿es grande tu familia?

LUISA: No, no es grande. Mi familia es pequeña. Aquí están mi papá, Juan Escobar, y mi mamá, María Ruiz de Escobar.

EDUARDO: ¡Hola! ¿Cómo están ustedes?

LUISA: Y aquí están mis tíos. Mi tía se llama Yolanda y mi tío se llama Rafael. ¡Oh, aquí están mis abuelos! Mi abuelo se llama don Chucho. Mi abuela se llama doña Alba.

EDUARDO: Buenas tardes, don Chucho. ¿Cómo está usted, doña Alba? Luisa, ¿tienes hermanos?

LUISA: ¡Claro que sí! Aquí están mi hermano Antonio, mi hermanita Ana, mi hermanito Paco, mi prima Josefa, mi primo...

EDUARDO: ¡Uf! ¿Ésta es una familia pequeña?

¿Cierto o falso?

[Each statement is given twice on the Test Cassette.]

1. Es la familia de Eduardo.
2. El papá se llama Juan.
3. El tío se llama Yolanda.
4. Doña Alba es la abuela.
5. Luisa tiene tres hermanos.

B. Dictado. Listen and write the missing words. You will hear each sentence twice.

[Each sentence is given twice on the Test Cassette.]

1. ¿Cómo se llama la hermanita de Carlos?
2. Se llama Mercedes. Tiene trece años.
3. ¿Cuántos hijos hay en la familia de Carlos?
4. Hay tres: Carlos, Eduardo y Mercedes.
5. Su familia no es muy grande.

C. Now try writing these sentences for extra credit. You will hear each sentence twice.

[Read each of the following sentences twice.]

ROSITA: ¡Buenos días, tío Juan!

JUAN: Buenos días, Rosita.

ROSITA: ¿Cómo está mi tía?

JUAN: Está muy bien.

ROSITA: ¡Tía Elena! ¡Qué gusto!

D. Listen carefully to these twelve words. You will hear each word twice. Complete each word by writing **p** or **t** on the answer blank. The first two have been done for you. (This test part is optional. Point values should not be applied to students' scores.)

1. ropa, ropa
2. rota, rota
3. gato, gato
4. sapo, sapo

5. prisa, prisa
6. tarde, tarde
7. español, español
8. tío, tío

9. historia, historia
10. porque, porque
11. divertido, divertido
12. patino, patino

END-OF-YEAR TEST [Test masters 112–113]

A. Listen to the conversation between Luis and Ana. Then you will hear five multiple-choice statements about their conversation. You will hear each statement twice. Circle the letter of the word or words that best complete each statement.

> LUIS: Ana, ¿qué hora es?
> ANA: Son las dos menos cinco, Luis.
> LUIS: ¡Adiós! Voy a ir a casa.
> ANA: ¿Por qué vas a ir a casa?
> LUIS: Porque tengo la gripe.
> ANA: ¿Cuándo tienes el examen de ciencias?
> LUIS: ¡En cinco minutos! No tengo la gripe, Ana. ¡Tengo miedo!
> ANA: ¿Miedo? ¿Por qué?
> LUIS: Porque no estudio. Los libros son aburridos.
> ANA: Mm… Ahora comprendo.

[Each multiple-choice statement is given twice on the Test Cassette.]

1. Son las dos menos…
  a. cuatro.
  b. cuarto.
  c. cinco.

2. Luis va a ir…
  a. a casa.
  b. a la escuela.
  c. al cine.

3. Luis no tiene la gripe. Él tiene…
  a. suerte.
  b. miedo.
  c. hambre.

4. Luis tiene examen de…
  a. ciencias.
  b. matemáticas.
  c. música.

5. Luis…
  a. no baila.
  b. no patina.
  c. no estudia.

B. Dictado. Listen carefully to these sentences. You will hear each sentence twice. Write the missing words on the answer blanks.

[Each sentence is given twice on the Test Cassette.]

1. El muchacho se llama David.
2. ¿Adónde va David?
3. Él va a sus clases favoritas.
4. Son las clases de inglés y español.
5. David es un buen alumno.

C. Listen carefully to these words. You will hear each word twice. Complete each word by writing a vowel or consonant letter on the answer blank. The first two have been done for you. (This test part is optional. Point values should not be applied to students' scores.)

1. prima, prima
2. pierna, pierna
3. abrigo, abrigo
4. medianoche, medianoche

5. rubio, rubio
6. cómica, cómica
7. jueves, jueves
8. que, que

9. mañana, mañana
10. zapatos, zapatos
11. lacio, lacio
12. cintura, cintura

ANSWER KEY

In this section, you will find the answers to all the tests in the *¡Hola!* *Testing Program* blackline master book. For each test, the following information is given: the test blackline master numbers, the total points for the test, and the section-by-section and part-by-part breakdown of points.

In addition, the levels of difficulty are provided for the unit tests, the achievement review tests, and the Mid-Year Test:

○ Lowest level of difficulty

◑ Average level of difficulty

● Highest level of difficulty

The following symbols are given for your information:

★ Extra credit

  Test Cassette

The complete tapescript for the Test Cassette is included in this *Testing Program* book in the section "Oral Test Tapescript and Guide." Also in that section you will find the information, or script, you will need to administer the Speaking Section of the Placement Test and the extra-credit parts in Section 3 of the unit tests (see Pages T-23 to T-53).

PLACEMENT TEST

(Test masters 1–8)

Total points: 60 / Total optional points: 10

Section 1

(15 points)

A. (5 points)

1. b (Es un loro.) *(model)*
2. c (Son las cinco y cuarto.)
3. e (¿Qué día es hoy?)
4. d (Es el mes de octubre.)
5. a (Hace mucho viento.)
6. f (Tengo ochenta años.)

B. (5 points)

1. cantar *(model)*
2. mesa
3. blanco
4. cuarenta y dos
5. difícil
6. biblioteca

C. (5 points)

1. negro *(model)*
2. abuelos
3. clase
4. globo
5. hambre
6. divertido

Section 2

(20 points)

A. (5 points)

1. Los perros son negros. *(model)*
2. Los pupitres son pequeños.
3. Son unos hijos divertidos.
4. Son unas mariposas amarillas.
5. Sus nietas son interesantes.
6. Los gatos son blancos.

B. (7 points)

1. usted *(model)*
2. le
3. Tú
4. Usted
5. Te
6. le
7. ella
8. Yo

C. (8 points)

1. estudio
2. escribe
3. lees
4. es
5. tengo
6. comprende
7. voy
8. hablas

Section 3

(25 points)

A. (5 points)

1. b (A Carlos le gusta *la clase de español.*)
2. c (El pupitre de Carlos es *pequeño.*)
3. a (La clase de inglés de Carlos es *terrible.*)
4. b (El salón número 15 no tiene *pupitres.*)
5. c (A Carlos le gusta mucho *el salón número 15.*)

B. (10 points)

1. ratón / pequeño
2. me / gustan
3. tengo / gatos
4. El gato negro tiene ojos amarillos.
5. El gato gris tiene ojos azules.

C. Speaking (10 points)

Answers will vary.

D. (10 optional points)

1. ha<u>c</u>e *(model)*
2. ga<u>t</u>o *(model)*
3. na<u>d</u>ar
4. suer<u>t</u>e
5. n<u>o</u>che
6. <u>i</u>nglés
7. ore<u>j</u>a
8. nunc<u>a</u>
9. a<u>b</u>urrido
10. llue<u>v</u>e
11. a<u>ñ</u>o
12. g<u>u</u>sta

(Test masters 9–15)

Total points: 50 / Total extra credit points: 10 / Total optional points: 10

Section 1

(15 points)

A. (4 points) ○
1. d (un lápiz)
2. c (una hoja de papel)
3. b (un libro)
4. a (un reloj)

B. (6 points) ○
1. b (mesa)
2. a (cuaderno)
3. g (ventana)
4. d (bandera)
5. c (pupitre)
6. f (bolígrafo)

C. (5 points) ◑
1. hombre *(model)*
2. mapa
3. borrador
4. tiza
5. regla
6. globo

Section 2

(20 points; 5 points extra credit)

A. (8 points) ○
1. la
2. el
3. el
4. la
5. las
6. los
7. los
8. las

B. (7 points) ○
1. libros
2. sillas
3. escritorios
4. hombres
5. borradores
6. paredes
7. ventanas

C. (5 points) ◑
1. el reloj
2. las banderas
3. el mapa
4. el pupitre
5. los cuadrados

D. (5 points) ● ★
1. mujeres hay?
2. alumnos hay?
3. sillas hay?
4. parades hay?
5. borradores hay?

Section 3

(15 points; 5 points extra credit)

A. (5 points) ◑
1. Cierto
2. Cierto
3. Falso
4. Falso
5. Cierto

B. (10 points) ◑
1. es *(model)*
2. de
3. Se
4. señor
5. Está
6. cuadernos
7. globo
8. dos
9. hay
10. muchacho
11. llamo

C. (5 points) ● ★
1. La muchacha se llama Juana.
2. Hay seis bolígrafos en la mesa.
3. La pizarra está en el salón de clase.
4. Hay un mapa en la pared.
5. Hay tres libros, profesora.

D. (10 optional points) ○
1. (adiós) *(model)*
2. (pronto) *(model)*
3. (mesa)
4. (bueno)
5. (nada)
6. (computadora)
7. (perro)
8. (deportes)
9. (bolígrafo)
10. (boxeo)
11. (cine)
12. (estás)

(Test masters 16–23)

Total points: 50 / Total extra credit points: 10 / Total optional points: 10

Section 1
(15 points)

A. (4 points) ○
1. d (rectángulo)
2. c (triángulo)
3. b (círculo)
4. a (cuadrado)

B. (5 points) ○
1. c (tigre) *(model)*
2. b (loro)
3. e (mariposa)
4. a (perro)
5. g (conejo)
6. d (pez)

C. (6 points) ◑
1. canario / amarillo
2. flamenco / rosado
3. ratón / blanco

Section 2
(20 points; 5 points extra credit)

A. (8 points) ○
1. un
2. un
3. unas
4. unos
5. unos
6. un
7. unos
8. una

B. (12 points) ◑
1. pájaro grande
2. pájaros pequeños
3. oso negro
4. osos blancos
5. regla larga
6. reglas cortas

C. (5 points) ● ★
1. animal *(model)*
2. oso
3. osos
4. grandes
5. canarios
6. amarillo

Section 3
(15 points; 5 points extra credit)

A. (5 points) ◑
1. Falso
2. Cierto
3. Cierto
4. Falso
5. Cierto

B. (10 points) ◑
1. círculo / pequeño
2. rectángulo / grande
3. Hasta / luego
4. triángulo / azul
5. profesora / gracias

C. (5 points) ● ★
1. ¿Cómo es el conejo?
2. El conejo es pequeño.
3. ¿Cuál es tu animal favorito?
4. Mi animal favorito es el flamenco.
5. ¿De qué color es?

D. (10 optional points) ○
1. (lib**r**os) *(model)*
2. (c**l**ase) *(model)*
3. (**a**marilla)
4. (señ**o**r)
5. (ra**t**ones)
6. (Espa**ñ**a)
7. (**B**olivia)
8. (nuest**r**a)
9. (v**o**tar)
10. (vam**o**s)
11. (cla**r**o)
12. (g**a**to)

UNIDAD 3: UNIT TEST

(Test masters 24–31)

Total points: 50 / Total extra credit points: 10 / Total optional points: 10

Section 1

(15 points)

A. (7 points) ○
1. domingo
2. miércoles
3. lunes
4. sábado
5. martes
6. jueves
7. viernes

B. (4 points) ○
1. cine
2. casa
3. escuela
4. clase

C. (4 points) ◑
1. Cierto
2. Falso
3. Falso
4. Cierto

Section 2

(20 points; 5 points extra credit)

A. (6 points) ○
1. va
2. Vas
3. Voy
4. Vas
5. Voy
6. Va

B. (6 points) ◑
1. a la
2. a la
3. a la
4. al
5. al
6. a la

C. (8 points) ◑
1. la
2. los
3. el
4. el
5. Los
6. el
7. los / la

D. (5 points) ● ★
1. Los lunes voy a la escuela.
2. Los martes voy a la clase de piano.
3. Los miércoles voy a la casa de Ana.
4. Los jueves voy a la clase.
5. Los viernes voy al cine.

Section 3

(15 points; 5 points extra credit)

A. (5 points) ◑
1. Cierto
2. Falso
3. Cierto
4. Cierto
5. Falso

B. (10 points) ◑
1. día / el
2. dos / jueves
3. Vas / la
4. voy / la
5. va / la

C. (5 points) ● ★
1. ¿Quién es esta muchacha?
2. No hay calendario.
3. ¿Adónde va Paco?
4. Carmen va a casa.
5. Esta semana no hay clase.

D. (10 optional points) ○
1. Ern_e_sto *(model)*
2. _u_na *(model)*
3. l_u_nes
4. mart_e_s
5. cin_e_
6. juev_e_s
7. l_u_na
8. az_u_l
9. _u_va
10. s_e_mana
11. _e_sta
12. ¿adónd_e_?

RePaso: Unidades 1–3 Achievement Review Test

(Test masters 32–36)

Total points: 40 / Total optional points: 10

Section 1
(10 points)

A. (5 points) ○
1. f (tigre) *(model)*
2. e (pequeño)
3. b (cine)
4. a (bolígrafo)
5. d (negro)
6. c (cuadrado)

B. (5 points) ◐
1. el oso *(model)*
2. el flamenco
3. la tiza
4. el globo
5. el canario
6. el hombre

Section 2
(15 points)

A. (12 points) ○
1. unas ventanas
2. unos libros pequeños
3. unos escritorios
4. las sillas
5. los osos negros

B. (3 points) ◐
1. voy *(model)*
2. va
3. Voy
4. vas

Section 3
(15 points)

A. (5 points) ◐
1. Cierto
2. Cierto
3. Falso
4. Cierto
5. Falso

B. (10 points) ●
1. muchacha / llama
2. triángulo / pequeño
3. quince / viernes
4. ¿Quién va a casa?
5. Hay un mapa en la mesa.

C. (10 optional points) ○
1. g<u>a</u>to *(model)*
2. p<u>e</u>z
3. osc<u>u</u>ro
4. <u>o</u>so
5. ¿adónd<u>e</u>?
6. v<u>o</u>y
7. pl<u>u</u>ma
8. vent<u>a</u>na
9. sill<u>a</u>
10. b<u>o</u>lígrafo
11. cin<u>e</u>

UNIDAD 4: UNIT TEST

(Test masters 37–44)

Total points: 50 / Total extra credit points: 10 / Total optional points: 10

Section 1

(15 points)

A. (5 points) ○
1. b (Voy a la casa.) *(model)*
2. c (Voy a la clase de música.)
3. f (Voy al gimnasio.)
4. e (Voy a la biblioteca.)
5. d (Voy a la clase de arte.)
6. a (Voy a la clase de computadoras.)

B. (5 points) ◐
1. e (ir al cine) *(model)*
2. f (usar la computadora)
3. c (cantar)
4. d (estudiar)
5. a (pintar)
6. b (practicar los deportes)

C. (5 points) ●
1. ir a la escuela *(model)*
2. practicar los deportes
3. usar la computadora
4. cantar
5. pintar
6. estudiar

Section 2

(20 points; 5 points extra credit)

A. (6 points) ◐
1. canta
2. Pintas
3. pinta
4. Estudias
5. estudia
6. Canto

B. (14 points) ◐
1. Vas a estudiar.
2. Voy a pintar.
3. va a practicar
4. Vas a usar
5. va a cantar
6. Voy a estudiar.
7. Vas a pintar.

C. (5 points) ● ★
Answers will vary.

Section 3

(15 points; 5 points extra credit)

A. (5 points) ◐
1. b (Pablo va *a las clases.*)
2. c (Pablo canta *muy bien.*)
3. a (Teresa va *al gimnasio.*)
4. c (Pablo va a usar *la computadora.*)
5. b (Teresa es *alumna.*)

B. (10 points) ◐
1. muy / bien
2. Cantas / clase
3. usa / computadora
4. va / estudiar
5. ir / cine

C. (5 points) ● ★
1. ¿Qué vas a hacer el lunes?
2. Mañana es domingo, ¿no?
3. ¿Qué hace Paula en la escuela?
4. ¡Es una muchacha pequeña!
5. Hay cuatro libros en el salón de clase.

D. (10 optional points) ○
1. (escuela) *(model)*
2. (pintas) *(model)*
3. (tiza)
4. (libro)
5. (deportes)
6. (usar)
7. (cinco)
8. (mira)
9. (Tomás)
10. (amarillo)
11. (arte)
12. (Isidro)

(Test masters 45–52)

Total points: 50 / Total extra credit points: 10 / Total optional points: 10

Section 1

(15 points)

A. (4 points) ○
1. la primavera
2. el invierno
3. el otoño
4. el verano

B. (8 points) ◐
1. j (Hace sol.)
2. g (Está nublado.)
3. e (Hace viento.)
4. i (Está lloviendo.)
5. h (Está nevando.)
6. d (Hace frío.)
7. f (Hace fresco.)
8. b (Hace mal tiempo.)

C. (3 points) ◐
1. el invierno
2. la primavera
3. el otoño

Section 2

(20 points; 5 points extra credit)

A. (5 points) ○
1. me *(model)*
2. le
3. Te
4. Te
5. le
6. me

B. (12 points) ◐
1. ¿Te gusta la computadora grande o la ~~computadora~~ pequeña?
   Me gusta la ~~computadora~~ grande.
2. ¿Cuál te gusta, la biblioteca grande o la ~~biblioteca~~ pequeña?
   Me gusta la ~~biblioteca~~ pequeña.
3. ¿Te gusta el gato blanco o el ~~gato~~ gris?
   Me gusta el ~~gato~~ gris.
4. ¿Te gusta la bandera verde o la ~~bandera~~ azul?
   Me gusta la ~~bandera~~ azul.
5. ¿Cuál te gusta más, el perro amarillo o el ~~perro~~ negro?
   Me gusta más el ~~perro~~ negro.
6. ¿Cuál te gusta más, la pluma roja o la ~~pluma~~ amarilla?
   Me gusta más la ~~pluma~~ roja.

C. (3 points) ◐
1. No, no le gusta.
2. Sí, le gusta.
3. Sí, le gusta.

D. (5 points) ● ★
Answers will vary.

Section 3

(15 points; 5 points extra credit)

A. (5 points) ◐
1. c (A Daniel le gusta *el verano.*)
2. a (A Daniel no le gusta *el invierno.*)
3. b (En el otoño hace *viento.*)
4. b (En la primavera hace *fresco.*)
5. a (Ahora está *lloviendo.*)

B. (10 points) ◐
1. una / larga
2. Cuántas / azules
3. gusta / cantar
4. calor / verano
5. está / nevando

C. (5 points) ●
1. ¿Cuáles son las estaciones?
2. ¿Qué te gusta hacer?
3. En la primavera llueve.
4. Hace muy buen tiempo hoy.
5. ¿No te gusta el invierno?

D. (10 optional points) ○
1. <u>e</u>stación *(model)*
2. n<u>a</u>cer *(model)*
3. gust<u>a</u>
4. inviern<u>o</u>
5. pr<u>i</u>mavera
6. ll<u>u</u>via
7. hac<u>e</u>
8. of<u>i</u>cina
9. nunc<u>a</u>
10. fresc<u>o</u>
11. est<u>u</u>dio
12. c<u>a</u>lor

UNIDAD 6: UNIT TEST

(Test masters 53–60)

Total points: 50 / Total extra credit points: 10 / Total optional points: 10

Section 1

(15 points)

A. (11 points) ○
1. e (mayo) *(model)*
2. g (julio)
3. b (febrero)
4. l (diciembre)
5. j (octubre)
6. a (enero)
7. c (marzo)
8. i (septiembre)
9. h (agosto)
10. k (noviembre)
11. d (abril)
12. f (junio)

B. (4 points) ○
1. patinar
2. caminar
3. bailar
4. nadar

Section 2

(20 points; 5 points extra credit)

A. (5 points) ○
1. patina *(model)*
2. estudia
3. pinta
4. nada
5. baila
6. camina

B. (10 points) ◑
JUAN:
¿<u>Tú</u> bailas bien? *(model)*
MARÍA:
¿Yo? Sí, <u>yo</u> bailo muy bien.

JUAN:
¿Miguel baila bien?
MARÍA:
No, <u>él</u> no baila bien.
JUAN:
¿Mariela baila mucho?
MARÍA:
Sí, <u>ella</u> baila mucho.
JUAN:
Señor Rivas, ¿<u>usted</u> baila?
SR. RIVAS:
Sí, <u>yo</u> bailo mucho.
JUAN:
¿Usted baila en casa?
SR. RIVAS:
No, <u>yo</u> no bailo en casa.
JUAN:
¿Canta <u>usted</u>?
SR. RIVAS:
Sí, <u>yo</u> canto.
MARÍA:
¿Canta la señora Rivas?
SR. RIVAS:
Sé, <u>ella</u> canta bien.
MARÍA:
¿Canta Alicia?
SR. RIVAS:
No, <u>ella</u> no canta.

C. (5 points) ◑
1. a veces
2. siempre
3. nunca
4. nunca
5. siempre

D. (5 points) ◑ ★
1. pinto
2. nada
3. bailas
4. patina
5. camina

Section 3

(15 points; 5 points extra credit)

A. (5 points) ◑
1. Cierto
2. Falso
3. Cierto
4. Cierto
5. Falso

B. (10 points) ◑
1. Te / nadar
2. Sí / me
3. mucho / mayo
4. Nado / julio
5. Qué / octubre

C. (5 points) ● ★
1. ¿Quién pinta?
2. Yo pinto muy bien.
3. ¿Pinta Isabel?
4. No, ella no pinta.
5. Rita pinta muy bien.

D. (10 optional points) ○
1. m<u>a</u>rzo *(model)*
2. <u>e</u>nero *(model)*
3. t<u>e</u>
4. <u>a</u>gosto
5. pa<u>t</u>inar
6. hac<u>e</u>
7. diciembr<u>e</u>
8. c<u>a</u>minar
9. n<u>a</u>dar
10. s<u>e</u>ptiembre
11. bail<u>a</u>r
12. v<u>e</u>rano

(Test masters 61–66)

Total points: 40 / Total optional points: 10

Section 1

(10 points)

A. (5 points) ○
1. diciembre *(model)*
2. invierno
3. arte
4. computadoras
5. biblioteca
6. casa

B. (5 points) ◐
1. pintar *(model)*
2. cantar
3. sol
4. lloviendo
5. bailar
6. patinar

Section 2

(15 points)

A. (5 points) ○
1. canta *(model)*
2. le
3. a la
4. al
5. estudio
6. nunca

B. (5 points) ◐
1. Voy *(model)*
2. va
3. Voy
4. Vas
5. Vas
6. va

C. (5 points) ●
ELENA:
¿T<u>ú</u> cantas bien? *(model)*
JORGE:
¿Yo? No, <u>yo</u> no canto. *(model)*
ELENA:
¿Ana canta bien?
JORGE:
Sí, <u>ella</u> canta muy bien.
ELENA:
¿José canta bien?
JORGE:
No, <u>él</u> no canta.
ELENA:
Señor García, ¿<u>usted</u> canta?
SR. GARCÍA:
Sí, <u>yo</u> canto mucho.
ELENA:
Señora Borges, ¿<u>usted</u> canta?
SRA. BORGES:
Sí, me gusta mucho cantar.

Section 3

(15 points)

A. (5 points) ◐
1. Cierto
2. Falso
3. Cierto
4. Cierto
5. Falso

B. (10 points) ●
1. le / cantar
2. Ella / música
3. Me / computadora
4. Ahora voy a la clase de arte.
5. Me gusta pintar.

C. (10 optional points) ○
1. cin<u>e</u> *(model)*
2. p<u>i</u>ntar *(model)*
3. dep<u>o</u>rtes
4. <u>g</u>usta
5. s<u>o</u>l
6. pat<u>i</u>nar
7. c<u>a</u>sa
8. m<u>u</u>cho
9. art<u>e</u>
10. d<u>i</u>ciembre
11. inviern<u>o</u>
12. est<u>u</u>dio

Mid-Year Test

Section 1
(15 points)

A. (5 points) ○
1. b (Hace mucho viento.) *(model)*
2. f (Es un hombre.)
3. e (Es una pared.)
4. c (Es un oso.)
5. a (La mariposa es grande.)
6. d (Es el número cincuenta y tres.)

B. (5 points) ◐
1. otoño *(model)*
2. cine
3. casa
4. fin de semana
5. pintar
6. arte

C. (5 points) ◐
1. verano.
2. sol.
3. nublado.
4. nadar.
5. agosto.

Section 2
(20 points)

A. (5 points) ○
1. Los loros son verdes. *(model)*
2. Las paredes son blancas.
3. Los gatos son grandes.
4. Son unos cuadernos.
5. Son unas ventanas.
6. Las mariposas son azules.

B. (7 points) ◐
1. usted *(model)*
2. te
3. me
4. Él
5. Tú
6. le
7. Yo
8. ella

C. (8 points) ◐
1. canta
2. bailas
3. voy
4. gusta
5. pinta
6. baila
7. vas
8. canto

Section 3
(15 points)

A. (5 points) ◐
1. b (Ahora hace mucho *frío*.)
2. a (A Ernesto no le gusta *el invierno*.)
3. c (A Ernesto le gusta *el calor*.)
4. a (En verano, Clarita va a *estudiar*.)
5. c (La clase de computadoras es muy *larga*.)

B. (10 points) ●
1. cuatro / mesa
2. Dónde
3. Hace / tiempo
4. Ella nada en el verano.
5. ¿No va a la escuela hoy?

C. (10 optional points) ○
1. agosto *(model)*
2. invierno *(model)*
3. hace
4. oscuro
5. largo
6. domingo
7. música
8. azul
9. esta
10. gimnasio
11. mayo
12. pluma

UNIDAD 7: UNIT TEST

(Test masters 75–81)

Total points: 50 / Total extra credit points: 10 / Total optional points: 10

Section 1
(15 points)

A. (5 points) ○
1. sed *(model)*
2. sueño
3. frío
4. hambre
5. calor
6. prisa

B. (5 points) ◑
1. Tengo suerte. *(model)*
2. Tengo dolor.
3. Tengo miedo.
4. Tengo la gripe.
5. Tengo ochenta años.
6. Tengo razón.

C. (5 points) ●
¿Cuántos años tienes?
Tengo _____ . (Answers will vary.
Students will write their ages.)

Section 2
(20 points; 5 points extra credit)

A. (6 points) ○
1. tiene
2. tengo
3. tienes
4. tengo
5. tienes
6. tengo

B. (7 points) ◑
1. usted *(model)*
2. tú
3. usted
4. tú
5. tú
6. tú
7. tú (OR usted)
8. tú

C. (7 points) ◑
1. usted
2. tú
3. tú
4. usted
5. tú
6. tú
7. usted

D. (5 points) ● ★
1. tiene
2. tienes
3. tienes
4. tiene
5. tengo

Section 3
(15 points; 5 points extra credit)

A. (5 points) ◑
1. Cierto
2. Cierto
3. Falso
4. Cierto
5. Falso

B. (10 points) ◑
1. Cuántos / señorita
2. Alicia / quince
3. Le / escuela
4. Sí / estudiar
5. Ella / libros

C. (5 points) ●
1. ¿Tienes hambre?
2. No, no tengo hambre.
3. ¿Tienes calor?
4. Sí, tengo mucho calor.
5. ¡Muchacha, tú tienes la gripe!

D. (10 optional points) ○
1. l<u>e</u>che *(model)*
2. c<u>i</u>nco *(model)*
3. v<u>i</u>ven
4. v<u>e</u>mos
5. p<u>e</u>so
6. p<u>i</u>so
7. pr<u>i</u>sa
8. s<u>e</u>d
9. gr<u>i</u>pe
10. herv<u>i</u>da
11. tr<u>e</u>s
12. suert<u>e</u>

UNIDAD 8: UNIT TEST

(Test masters 82–90)
Total points: 50 / Total extra credit points: 10 / Total optional points: 10

Section 1
(15 points)

A. (3 points) ○
1. la salida del sol *(model)*
2. la puesta del sol
3. el mediodía
4. la medianoche

B. (3 points) ◑
1. un minuto *(model)*
2. una media hora
3. un cuarto de hora
4. una hora

C. (3 points) ●
1. la mañana *(model)*
2. punto
3. la tarde
4. la noche

D. (6 points) ●
1. Cómo *(model)*
2. Cuántos
3. Adónde
4. Quién
5. Qué
6. Cuándo
7. Cuál

Section 2
(20 points; 5 points extra credit)

A. (8 points) ○
1. Es / y *(model)*
2. Son / y
3. Son / menos
4. Son / menos
5. Es / y
6. Son / y
7. Son / menos
8. Son / menos
9. Es / y

B. (7 points) ○
1. Cómo *(model)*
2. Qué
3. Cuál
4. Adónde
5. qué
6. Cuántos
7. Cuándo
8. Quién

C. (5 points) ◑
1. Son las diez y doce. *(model)*
2. Son las nueve y veinte.
3. Son las ocho menos cuarto.
4. Son las cinco y diez.
5. Son las cuatro menos cinco.
6. Es la una y media.

D. (5 points) ● ★
Answers will vary.

Section 3
(15 points; 5 points extra credit)

A. (5 points) ◑
1. Cierto
2. Cierto
3. Falso
4. Falso
5. Cierto

B. (10 points) ◑
1. va / ocho
2. le / estudiar
3. cuatro / punto
4. estudia / horas
5. nueve / noche

C. (5 points) ● ★
1. ¿Cuántos minutos hay en media hora?
2. Hay treinta minutos.
3. ¿Cuántos minutos hay en un cuarto de hora?
4. Hay quince minutos.
5. Muchas gracias, profesora.

D. (10 optional points) ○
1. hora *(model)*
2. minuto *(model)*
3. cuarto
4. una
5. punto
6. sol
7. mula
8. noche
9. ¿cuándo?
10. ¿cómo?
11. gusta
12. mucho

(Test masters 91–98)

Total points: 50 / Total extra credit points: 10 / Total optional points: 10

Section 1

(15 points)

A. (7 points) ○
1. h (educación física) *(model)*
2. e (inglés)
3. a (ciencias)
4. g (salud)
5. d (español)
6. f (ciencias sociales)
7. c (matemáticas)
8. b (geografía)

B. (7 points) ◑
1. Es divertido. *(model)*
2. Es fácil.
3. Es difícil.
4. ¡Es terrible!
5. ¡Es fantástico!
6. Es interesante.
7. Es aburrido.
8. Es importante.

C. (1 point) ●
DANIEL:
¿Por qué?

Section 2

(20 points; 5 points extra credit)

A. (4 points) ○
ALICIA:
Me gustan las ciencias sociales. *(model)*
CARLOS:
¿Te gustan las matemáticas?

ALICIA:
Sí, y me gustan las ciencias.
CARLOS:
¿Te gusta la educación física?
ALICIA:
No, no me gustan los deportes.

B. (5 points) ◑
SAMUEL:
Señor Martí, ¿le gustan los perros? *(model)*
SR. MARTÍ:
No, no me gustan los perros. Los gatos, sí. Me gustan los gatos.
JUANITA:
Samuel, ¿te gustan los gatos?
SAMUEL:
No. Alicia tiene un gato. No me gustan los gatos.
JUANITA:
Pues, y también tengo un gato. Se llama Dot. Me gusta mucho Dot.

C. (11 points) ◑
(leer)
1. LUIS:
Yo leo español. *model)*
ANA:
Tú lees inglés, ¿no?
LUIS:
Sí. Mi amigo Daniel lee inglés y español.

(aprender)
2. JULIO:
¿Qué aprende Ana en la clase de ciencias?

ANITA:
Ella aprende mucho en la clase de ciencias.
JULIO:
¿Qué aprendes tú en la clase de matemáticas?

(escribir)
3. JOSÉ:
Alejandro escribe bien.
HUGO:
José, ¿tú escribes bien?
JOSÉ:
Sí, yo escribo bien.

(comprender)
4. DIANA:
Yo no comprendo a Carlos.
PACO:
Carlos no comprende a Sara.
DIANA:
Tú no comprendes a Carlos.

D. (5 points) ◑ ★
SARA:
Yo no aprendo mucho en la clase de inglés. *(model)* No comprendo al profesor.
ROSA:
¡Qué lástima! ¿Lees tú el libro?
SARA:
Sí, leo el libro y escribo mucho. Voy a hablar con el profesor.
ROSA:
Buena idea. Él va a comprender.

Section 3

(15 points; 5 points extra credit)

A. (5 points)

1. Cierto
2. Falso
3. Falso
4. Cierto
5. Cierto

B. (10 points)

1. Aprendo / escuela
2. Los / fantásticos
3. muy
4. Tengo / importantes
5. español
6. gusta / física

C. (5 points) ● ★

1. ¿Por qué estudias español?
2. Porque me gusta.
3. ¿Dónde estudias?
4. En la escuela y en casa.
5. El español es muy divertido.

D. (10 optional points) ○

1. sí (día) *(model)*
2. no (terrible) *(model)*
3. sí (usted) *(model)*
4. sí (dolor)
5. sí (aburrido)
6. no (vivo)
7. sí (difícil)
8. sí (salud)
9. no (inglés)
10. sí (educación)
11. no (hora)
12. sí (verdad)
13. no (importante)

UNIDAD 10: UNIT TEST

(Test masters 99–105)

Total points: 50 / Total extra credit points: 10 / Total optional points: 10

Section 1

(15 points)

A. (10 points) ○
1. bisabuelo *(model)*
2. bisabuela
3. abuelo
4. abuela
5. papá
6. mamá
7. tío
8. tía
9. hermano
10. primo
11. prima

B. (5 points) ◑
1. bisabuelos *(model)*
2. abuelos
3. papás
4. tíos
5. hermanos
6. primos

Section 2

(20 points; 5 points extra credit)

A. (11 points) ○
1. a. mi *(model)*
   b. mis
   c. mis
   d. mi
2. a. tu
   b. tu
   c. tus
   d. tus
3. a. su
   b. sus
   c. su
   d. sus

B. (9 points) ◑
1. mesita
2. globito
3. libritos
4. casitas
5. papelito
6. abuelito
7. hermanitos
8. hijitos
9. hermanita

C. (5 points) ● ★
1. Anita
2. Juanito
3. Ricardito
4. Sarita
5. Rosita

Section 3

(15 points; 5 points extra credit)

A. (5 points) ◑
1. Falso
2. Cierto
3. Falso
4. Cierto
5. Cierto

B. (10 points) ◑
1. Cómo / hermanita
2. Tiene / trece
3. hijos / hay
4. tres / y
5. Su / grande

C. (5 points) ● ★
ROSITA:
¡Buenos días, tío Juan!
JUAN:
Buenos días, Rosita.
ROSITA:
¿Cómo está mi tía?
JUAN:
¡Está muy bien!
ROSITA:
¡Tía Elena! ¡Qué gusto!

D. (10 optional points) ○
1. ro̲pa *(model)*
2. ro̲ta *(model)*
3. ga̲to
4. sa̲po
5. p̲risa
6. t̲arde
7. es̲pañol
8. t̲ío
9. his̲toria
10. p̲orque
11. diver̲tido
12. p̲atino

(Test masters 106–113)

Total points: 50 / Total optional points: 10

Section 1

(15 points)

A. (5 points)

1. b (Es una mujer.) *(model)*
2. f (Son las tres y media.)
3. c (¿Qué día es hoy?)
4. d (El mes es febrero.)
5. a (Está nevando.)
6. e (Tengo mucho calor.)

B. (5 points)

1. viento *(model)*
2. bandera
3. rosado
4. estudiar
5. fácil
6. abuelos

C. (5 points)

1. amarillo *(model)*
2. gimnasio
3. hambre
4. cuarto
5. treinta
6. setenta

Section 2

(20 points)

A. (5 points)

1. Los osos son blancos. *(model)*
2. Los borradores son pequeños.
3. Las banderas son rojas.
4. Son unos globos interesantes.
5. Son unas ventanas grandes.
6. Mis primas son divertidas.

B. (7 points)

1. tú *(model)*
2. Yo
3. usted
4. me
5. le
6. Su
7. él
8. mis

C. (8 points)

1. estudia
2. aprendo
3. escribes
4. son
5. tiene
6. gustan
7. va
8. lees

Section 3

(15 points)

A. (5 points)

1. c (Son las dos menos *cinco.*)
2. a (Luis va a ir *a casa.*)
3. b (Luis no tiene la gripe. Él tiene *miedo.*)
4. a (Luis tiene examen de *ciencias.*)
5. c (Luis *no estudia.*)

B. (10 points)

1. muchacho / llama
2. Adónde / va
3. Él / clases
4. Son las clases de inglés y español.
5. David es un buen alumno.

C. (10 optional points)

1. prima *(model)*
2. pierna *(model)*
3. abrigo
4. medianoche
5. rubio
6. cómica
7. jueves
8. que
9. mañana
10. zapatos
11. lacio
12. cintura

Teacher's Resource Charts

Blackline Masters

¡HOLA! STUDENT PROGRESS CHART

Student's Name _____ Grade _____

Vocabulary Sections (Section 1)

Test	Points	Points Earned	Comments	Date
Placement	15			
Unidad 1	15			
Unidad 2	15			
Unidad 3	15			
Repaso: Unidades 1–3	10			
Unidad 4	15			
Unidad 5	15			
Unidad 6	15			
Repaso: Unidades 4–6	10			
Mid-Year	15			
Unidad 7	15			
Unidad 8	15			
Unidad 9	15			
Unidad 10	15			
End-of-Year	15			
Total	**200**			

¡HOLA! STUDENT PROGRESS CHART

¡HOLA! STUDENT PROGRESS CHART

Student's Name _____ Grade _____

Structure Sections (Section 2)

Test	Points*	Points Earned	Comments	Date
Placement	20			
Unidad 1	20 (5)			
Unidad 2	20 (5)			
Unidad 3	20 (5)			
Repaso: Unidades 1–3	15			
Unidad 4	20 (5)			
Unidad 5	20 (5)			
Unidad 6	20 (5)			
Repaso: Unidades 4–6	15			
Mid-Year	20			
Unidad 7	20 (5)			
Unidad 8	20 (5)			
Unidad 9	20 (5)			
Unidad 10	20 (5)			
End-of-Year	20			
Total	270 (50)			

* Numbers in parentheses represent extra-credit points.

¡HOLA! STUDENT PROGRESS CHART

Student's Name _____   Grade _____

Oral Sections (Section 3)

Test	Points*	Points Earned	Comments	Date
Placement	25			
Unidad 1	15 (5)			
Unidad 2	15 (5)			
Unidad 3	15 (5)			
Repaso: Unidades 1–3	15			
Unidad 4	15 (5)			
Unidad 5	15 (5)			
Unidad 6	15 (5)			
Repaso: Unidades 4–6	15			
Mid-Year	15			
Unidad 7	15 (5)			
Unidad 8	15 (5)			
Unidad 9	15 (5)			
Unidad 10	15 (5)			
End-of-Year	15			
Total	**210 (50)**			

* Numbers in parentheses represent extra-credit points.

¡HOLA! COMPOSITE SCORE CHART

Student's Name _____   Grade _____

Test	Section	Subscores	Total Score	Date
Placement	Section 1	_____		_____
	Section 2	_____		_____
	Section 3	_____		_____
	Speaking	_____		_____
			_____	
Unidad **1**	Section 1	_____		_____
	Section 2	_____		_____
	Section 3	_____		_____
			_____	
Unidad **2**	Section 1	_____		_____
	Section 2	_____		_____
	Section 3	_____		_____
			_____	
Unidad **3**	Section 1	_____		_____
	Section 2	_____		_____
	Section 3	_____		_____
			_____	

¡HOLA! COMPOSITE SCORE CHART

Student's Name _____ Grade _____

Test	Section	Subscores	Total Score	Date
Repaso: Unidades 1–3	Section 1	_____		_____
	Section 2	_____		_____
	Section 3	_____		_____
			_____	
Unidad **4**	Section 1	_____		_____
	Section 2	_____		_____
	Section 3	_____		_____
			_____	
Unidad **5**	Section 1	_____		_____
	Section 2	_____		_____
	Section 3	_____		_____
			_____	
Unidad **6**	Section 1	_____		_____
	Section 2	_____		_____
	Section 3	_____		_____
			_____	
Repaso: Unidades 4–6	Section 1	_____		_____
	Section 2	_____		_____
	Section 3	_____		_____
			_____	

© National Textbook Company

¡HOLA! COMPOSITE SCORE CHART

Student's Name _____ Grade _____

Test	Section	Subscores	Total Score	Date
Mid-Year	Section 1	_____		_____
	Section 2	_____		_____
	Section 3	_____		_____
			_____	
Unidad **7**	Section 1	_____		_____
	Section 2	_____		_____
	Section 3	_____		_____
			_____	
Unidad **8**	Section 1	_____		_____
	Section 2	_____		_____
	Section 3	_____		_____
			_____	
Unidad **9**	Section 1	_____		_____
	Section 2	_____		_____
	Section 3	_____		_____
			_____	

¡HOLA! COMPOSITE SCORE CHART

Student's Name _____ Grade _____

Test	Section	Subscores	Total Score	Date
Unidad **10**	Section 1	_____		_____
	Section 2	_____		_____
	Section 3	_____		_____
			_____	
End-of-Year	Section 1	_____		_____
	Section 2	_____		_____
	Section 3	_____		_____
			_____	

STUDENT TESTS

Blackline Masters

Nombre _____

Section 1

A. Read the sentences in the list below. Then look at the pictures. Write the letter of each sentence on the answer blank under the picture it describes. The first one has been done for you.

a. Hace mucho viento.
b. Es un loro.
c. Son las cinco y cuarto.
d. Es el mes de octubre.
e. ¿Qué día es hoy?
f. Tengo ochenta años.

1.

b
_____

2.

_____

3. jueves

_____

4.

_____

5.

_____

6.

_____

Nombre _____

B. First, look at the picture. Then choose the word or phrase from the list that completes the sentence next to the picture. Write the word or phrase on the answer blank. The first one has been done for you.

biblioteca	difícil
cantar	blanco
cuarenta y dos	mesa

1.

Voy a __**cantar**__ .

2.

Es una

_____ .

3.

El ratón es

_____ .

4. **42** _____

_____

5.

Es

_____ .

6.

Voy a la

_____ .

¡HOLA!

Nombre _____

c. Look at each picture. Then, on the answer blank, write the word that completes the sentence next to the picture. The first one has been done for you.

1.  El oso es

   negro _____ .

2.  Son mis

   _____ .

3.  ¡Es una

   _____

   aburrida!

4.  Es el

   _____

   de Paula.

5.  Tengo

   _____ .

6.  Alfredo es

   _____ .

Nombre _____

Section 2

A. Each sentence below describes **one** person, animal, or thing. Read the sentence. Then, on the answer blank, write the sentence again, changing it to tell about **more than one** person, animal, or thing. The first one has been done for you.

One	More than one
One	**More than one**

1. El perro es negro.   **Los perros son negros** _____ .

2. El pupitre es pequeño. _____ .

3. Es un hijo divertido. _____ .

4. Es una mariposa amarilla. _____ .

5. Su nieta es interesante. _____ .

6. El gato es blanco. _____ .

B. Complete the following sentences, using words from the list below. The first one has been done for you.

| yo | él | usted | te |
| tú | ella | me | le |

1. Señora López, ¿ _____**usted**_____ tiene hijos?

2. A José _____ gustan los gatos.

3. ¿ _____ eres alumna?

¡HOLA!

Nombre _____

Part **B**, *continued.*

4. ¡Señora Vargas! ¡ _____ pinta muy bien!

5. Tú eres buena alumna. _____ gusta la escuela.

6. ¿A Inés _____ gustan los loros?

7. ¿Patina bien Isabel?

   Sí, _____ patina bien.

8. _____ canto muy bien.

C. Complete the sentences below by writing the correct form of the verb in parentheses on each answer blank.

[M] Isabel _____**canta**_____ bien.
   (cantar)

1. Yo _____ en casa.
   (estudiar)

2. Juan _____ en la pizarra.
   (escribir)

3. Tú _____ muchos libros.
   (leer)

➡

Nombre _____

Part **C**, *continued.*

4. Anita _____ mi hermana.
    (ser)

5. Yo _____ catorce años.
    (tener)

6. Liliana _____ la geografía.
    (comprender)

7. Mañana yo _____ a pintar.
    (ir)

8. ¿Tú _____ español?
    (hablar)

Nombre _____

Section 3

A. Listen to the conversation between Julia and Carlos. Then you will hear five multiple-choice statements about their conversation. You will hear each statement twice. Circle the letter of the word or phrase that best completes each statement.

1. a   b   c   **4.** a   b   c

2. a   b   c   **5.** a   b   c

3. a   b   c

B. Dictado. Listen carefully to these sentences. You will hear each sentence twice. Write the missing words on the answer blanks.

1. El _____ es un animal _____ .

2. No _____ _____ los ratones.

3. Yo _____ dos _____ .

4. _____ .

5. _____ .

C. This is a speaking test. Listen to your teacher's instructions.

PLACEMENT TEST

Nombre _____

D. Listen carefully to these words. You will hear each word twice. Complete each word by writing a vowel or consonant letter on the answer blank. The first two have been done for you. (This test part is optional. Point values should not be applied to students' scores.)

1. hac __e____

2. ga __t____ o

3. na _____ ar

4. suer _____ e

5. n _____ che

6. _____ nglés

7. ore _____ a

8. nunc _____

9. a _____ urrido

10. llue _____ e

11. a _____ o

12. g _____ sta

¡HOLA!

Nombre _____

Section 1

A. Read the words in the list. Then look at each picture below, and write **a, b, c,** or **d** on the answer blank to identify the picture.

---

    a. un reloj   **c.** una hoja de papel
    b. un libro   **d.** un lápiz

1. _____

2. _____

3. _____

4. _____

B. **¿Qué es?** Look at the picture on the next page. Then, in the list below, find the word that names it. Write the letter on the answer blank beside the picture. Follow the model.

---

    a. cuaderno   **c.** pupitre   **e.** cesta   **g.** ventana
    b. mesa   **d.** bandera   **f.** bolígrafo

➡️

Nombre _____

Part **B**, *continued.*

  e ___

a. cuaderno	**e.** cesta
b. mesa	**f.** bolígrafo
c. pupitre	**g.** ventana
d. bandera	

1.  ___

2.  ___

3. ___

4.  ___

5. ___

6. 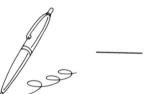 ___

C. Look at the picture. Then write the name of the object on the answer blank. The first one has been done for you.

1.

hombre
_____

2.
_____

3.
_____

4.
_____

5.
_____

6.
_____

¡HOLA!

Nombre _____

Section 2

A. Complete these sentences using **el, la, los,** or **las**.

 Es ___**el**___
cuaderno.

1. Es _____
profesora.

2. Es _____
alumno.

3. Es _____
reloj.

4.  Es _____
mujer.

5.  Son _____
profesoras.

6. Son _____
alumnos.

7. Son _____
relojes.

8. Son _____
mujeres.

Nombre _____

B. Change the underlined words to show that there are two of each.

| M | Hay una <u>alumna</u>. | Ahora hay dos | **alumnas** . |

1. Hay un <u>libro</u>.   Ahora hay dos _____.

2. Hay una <u>silla</u>.   Ahora hay dos _____.

3. Hay una <u>escritorio</u>.   Ahora hay dos _____.

4. Hay un <u>hombre</u>.   Ahora hay dos _____.

5. Hay un <u>borrador</u>.   Ahora hay dos _____.

6. Hay una <u>pared</u>.   Ahora hay dos _____.

7. Hay una <u>ventana</u>.   Ahora hay dos _____.

C. **¿Qué es?** Circle the words that complete each sentence.

M Es ((el alumno) los alumnos).

1. Es (el reloj, los relojes).

2. Son (la bandera, las banderas).

3. Es (el mapa, los mapas).

4. Es (el pupitre, los pupitres).

5. Son (el cuadrado, los cuadrados).

¡HOLA!

Nombre _____

★ **D.** For extra credit, complete the questions for these answers.

M ¿Cuántas ___**mesas hay?**_____
Hay tres mesas.

1. ¿Cuántas _____
Hay dos mujeres.

2. ¿Cuántos _____
Hay un alumno.

3. ¿Cuántas _____
Hay catorce sillas.

4. ¿Cuántas _____
Hay cuatro paredes.

5. ¿Cuántos _____
Hay tres borradores.

Nombre _____

Section 3

A. Listen to the conversation between Carlos and Olga. Then you will hear five statements about their conversation. You will hear each statement twice. Circle **CIERTO** if the statement is true. Circle **FALSO** if it is false.

1. CIERTO   FALSO

2. CIERTO   FALSO

3. CIERTO   FALSO

4. CIERTO   FALSO

5. CIERTO   FALSO

B. Dictado. Listen carefully to these sentences and phrases. You will hear each one twice. Write the missing word on the answer blank. The first one has been done for you.

1. ¿Qué _____**es**_____ esto?

2. el salón _____ clase

3. _____ llama David.

4. el _____ Rodríguez

5. ¿ _____ bien Olga?

6. Son los _____ .

7. Es el _____ .

8. ¿Hay _____ profesores?

Nombre _____

Part **B**, *continued.*

9. ¿Cuántos _____ ?

10. El _____ está muy bien.

11. Me _____ Carlos.

★ **C.** Now try writing these sentences for extra credit. You will hear each sentence twice.

1. _____ .

2. _____ .

3. _____ .

4. _____ .

5. _____ .

D. You will hear a number and a word. If the word contains an **a** sound, circle the number. If the word does not have an **a** sound, do not circle the number. The first two have been done for you. (This test part is optional. Point values should not be applied to students' scores.)

① (adiós) **5.**   **9.**

2. (pronto) **6.**   **10.**

3.   **7.**   **11.**

4.   **8.**   **12.**

Nombre _____

Section 1

A. What shape is it? Read the words in the list. Then look at each shape below and write **a, b, c,** or **d** on the answer blank to identify the shape.

a. cuadrado   c. triángulo

b. círculo   d. rectángulo

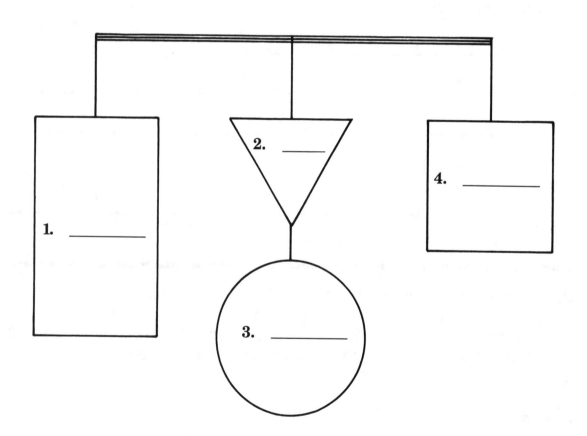

Nombre _____

B. **¿Qué es esto?** Look at each picture. Then find the word in the list that names the picture. Write the letter on the answer blank. The first one has been done for you.

a. perro	**c.** tigre	**e.** mariposa	**g.** conejo
b. loro	**d.** pez	**f.** pájaro	**h.** gato

1.  __c__

2.  _____

3.  _____

4.  _____

5.  _____

6.  _____

C. Look at the picture. Then read the list of colors. Write the name and the color of the animal on the answer blanks.

rosado	negro	blanco	amarillo

El ___**oso**___ es ___**negro**___.

UNIDAD 2 / EXAMEN

Nombre _____

Part **C**, continued.

rosado	negro	blanco	amarillo

1.

El _____ es _____ .

2.

El _____ es _____ .

3.

El _____ es _____ .

¡HOLA!

Nombre _____

Section 2

A. Complete the sentences below by writing **un, una, unos,** or **unas.**

M Hay ____un____ tigre.

1. Hay _____ canario.

2. Hay _____ perro.

3. Hay _____ mariposas.

4. Hay _____ gatos.

5. Hay _____ perros.

6. Hay _____ conejo.

7. Hay _____ conejos.

8. Hay _____ mariposa.

B. Use one word from **A** and one from **B** to label each picture.

A	B
mariposa	blancos
oso	cortas
osos	grande
pájaro	larga
pájaros	negro
regla	negra
reglas	pequeños

M  **mariposa negra** _____

Nombre _____

Part **B**, *continued*.

1.

   _____

2.

   _____

3.

   _____

4.

   _____

5.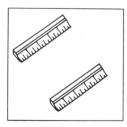

   _____

6.

   _____

A
mariposa
oso
osos
pájaro
pájaros
regla
reglas
B
blancos
cortas
grande
larga
negro
negra
pequeños

¡HOLA!

Nombre _____

★ **C.** Imagine that the bear is your favorite animal, but at home you can only have a canary. Complete these sentences for extra credit. The first answer blank has been filled in for you.

Mi ____**animal**____ favorito es el _____ .
       (1)   **(2)**

Los _____ son _____ y de color negro.
      (3)   **(4)**

En mi casa hay un canario. Los _____ son pequeños y de color
                                          (5)

_____ .
  (6)

Nombre _____

Section 3

A. Listen to the conversation between Ana and Marcos. Then you will hear five statements about their conversation. You will hear each statement twice. Circle **CIERTO** if the statement is true. Circle **FALSO** if it is false.

1. CIERTO   FALSO

2. CIERTO   FALSO

3. CIERTO   FALSO

4. CIERTO   FALSO

5. CIERTO   FALSO

B. Dictado. Listen to these sentences and write the missing words. You will hear each sentence twice.

1. El _____ es _____ .

2. El _____ es _____ .

3. ¡_____ _____!

4. El _____ es _____ .

5. Sí _____ . ¡Muchas _____!

Nombre _____

★ **C.** Now try writing these sentences for extra credit. You will hear each sentence twice.

1. _____

2. _____

3. _____

4. _____

5. _____

D. Listen carefully to these twelve words. You will hear each word twice. Complete each word by writing **a** or **o** on the answer blank. The first two have been done for you. (This test part is optional. Point values should not be applied to students' scores.)

1. libr __o__ s

2. cl __a__ se

3. _____ marilla

4. señ _____ r

5. rat _____ nes

6. Esp _____ ña

7. B _____ livia

8. nuestr _____

9. v _____ tar

10. vam _____ s

11. clar _____

12. g _____ to

Nombre _____

Section 1

A. Use the calendar below to complete the sentences.

lunes	martes	miércoles	jueves	viernes	sábado	domingo
				1	2	3
4	5	6	7	8	9	10
11	12	13	14	15	16	17
18	19	20	21	22	23	24
25	26	27	28	29	30	

M El día quince es ___**viernes**___ .

1. El día tres es _____ .

2. El día seis es _____ .

3. El día cuatro es _____ .

4. El día nueve es _____ .

5. El día doce es _____ .

6. El día siete es _____ .

7. El día ocho es _____ .

Nombre _____

B. Read the words in the list on the right. Then draw a line from each picture to the word that names it. Follow the model.

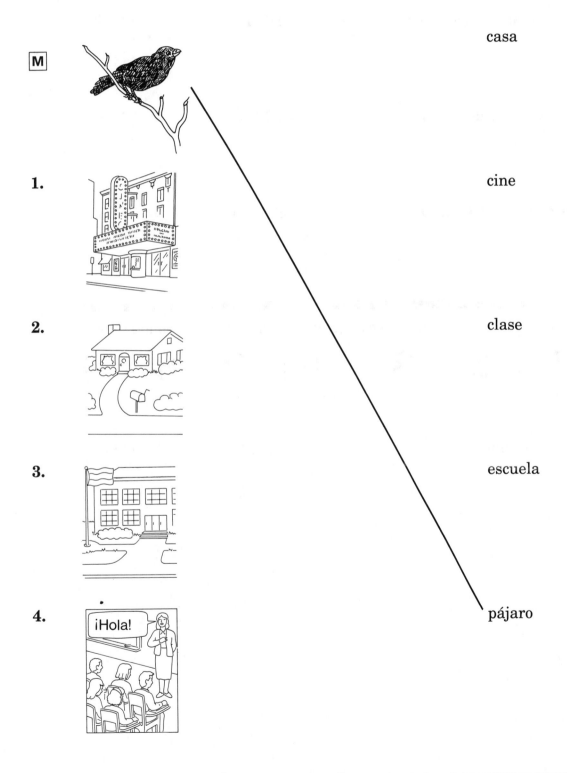

casa

M

1.

cine

2.

clase

3.

escuela

4. ¡Hola!

pájaro

Nombre _____

C. Read the sentences below. Circle **CIERTO** if the statement is true. Circle **FALSO** if the statement is false.

1. Hay siete días en una semana.   CIERTO   FALSO

2. El lunes es el fin de semana.   CIERTO   FALSO

3. Hoy es domingo. Hay clase.   CIERTO   FALSO

4.

lunes	martes	miércoles	jueves	viernes	sábado	domingo
1	2	3	4	5	6	7

El día tres es miércoles.   CIERTO   FALSO

Nombre _____

Section 2

A. Imagine that you are the person talking in each picture. Then, on the answer blank, complete each sentence, using **voy, vas,** or **va**.

_____**Va**_____ a la escuela.

1.

Juan _____ a la casa.

2.

_____ al cine.

3.

_____ a la escuela.

4.

_____ a la escuela.

5.

_____ a la casa.

6.

_____ al cine.

Nombre_____

B. Complete the sentences by writing **al** or **a la** on the answer blank.

M ¿Adónde va el muchacho?

El muchacho va ____al____ cine.

1. ¿Adónde va Pedro?

Pedro va _____ clase.

2. ¿Adónde vas tú?

Voy _____ escuela.

3. ¿Vas al cine?

No, voy _____ casa de José.

4. ¿Adónde va Luisa?

Ella va _____ salón de clase.

5. ¿Vas a la escuela?

No, voy _____ parque.

6. ¿Adónde vas mañana?

Voy _____ tienda.

C. Complete the sentences by writing **el, los, la,** or **las** on the answer blank.

M Eduardo va ____el____ lunes.

1. Emilio va _____ próxima semana.

2. Marta va _____ domingos.

Nombre _____

Part **C**, *continued.*

3. Alberto va _____ sábado.

4. ¿Qué día es _____ diez?

5. _____ sábados voy al cine.

6. ¿Cuándo es _____ fin de semana?

7. ¿Cuáles son _____ días de _____ semana?

★ **D.** For extra credit, write sentences that tell where you generally go on certain days.

M domingos / cine

Los domingos voy al cine.

1. lunes / escuela

_____

2. martes / clase de piano

_____

3. miércoles / casa de Ana

_____

4. jueves / clase

_____

5. viernes / cine

_____

Nombre _____

Section 3

A. Listen to the conversation between Carmen and Isidro. Then you will hear five statements about their conversation. You will hear each statement twice. Circle **CIERTO** if the statement is true. Circle **FALSO** if it is false.

1.   CIERTO   FALSO

2.   CIERTO   FALSO

3.   CIERTO   FALSO

4.   CIERTO   FALSO

5.   CIERTO   FALSO

B.   Dictado. Listen carefully to these sentences. You will hear each sentence twice. Write the missing words on the answer blanks.

1. ¿Qué _____ es _____ dos?

2. El _____ es _____ .

3. ¿ _____ a _____ escuela hoy?

4. No, no _____ a _____ escuela hoy.

5. Ella _____ a _____ casa de Carlos.

Nombre _____

★ **C.** Now try writing these sentences for extra credit. You will hear each sentence twice.

1. _____

2. _____

3. _____

4. _____

5. _____

D. Listen carefully to these twelve words. You will hear each word twice. Complete each word by writing **e** or **u** on the answer blank. The first two have been done for you. (This test part is optional. Point values should not be applied to students' scores.)

1. Ern __e__ sto

2. __u__ na

3. l ____ nes

4. mart ____ s

5. cin ____

6. juev ____ s

7. l ____ na

8. az ____ l

9. ____ va

10. s ____ mana

11. ____ sta

12. ¿adónd ____ ?

Nombre _____

Section 1

A. Read the words in the list. Then look at each picture. Find the word in the list that names or describes the picture and write the letter in the answer blank. The first one has been done for you.

---

a. bolígrafo	**c.** cuadrado	**e.** pequeño
b. cine	**d.** negro	**f.** tigre

1.

f _____

2.

_____

3.

_____

4.

_____

5.

_____

6.

_____

¡HOLA!

Nombre _____

B. Look at the picture. Then write the name of the object on the answer blank. The first one has been done for you.

1.

el oso
_____

2.

_____

3.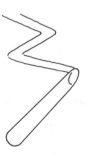

_____

4.

_____

5.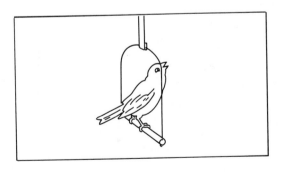

_____

6.

_____

Nombre _____

Section 2

A. Change the underlined words to show that there are more than one of each item.

M	Hay un gato.	Hay	**unos gatos** .
M	Es la pared.	Son	**las paredes** .
1.	Hay una ventana.	Hay	_____ .
2.	Hay un libro pequeño.	Hay	_____ .
3.	Hay un escritorio.	Hay	_____ .
4.	Es la silla.	Son	_____ .
5.	Es el oso negro.	Son	_____ .

B. Imagine that you are talking to your little brother Raúl. Complete your answers to his questions. The first one has been done for you.

1. RAÚL: ¿Vas a la casa?

   YOU: No, no _____**voy**_____ a la casa.

2. RAÚL: ¿Quién va a la casa?

   YOU: Susana _____ a la casa.

3. RAÚL: ¿Adónde vas?

   YOU: _____ al cine.

4. RAÚL: ¿No voy al cine?

   YOU: No, _____ a la casa.

Nombre _____

Section 3

A. Listen to the conversation between Paula and Miguel. Then you will hear five statements about their conversation. You will hear each statement twice. Circle **CIERTO** if the statement is true. Circle **FALSO** if it is false.

1. CIERTO   FALSO

2. CIERTO   FALSO

3. CIERTO   FALSO

4. CIERTO   FALSO

5. CIERTO   FALSO

B. Dictado. Listen to these sentences and write the missing words. You will hear each sentence twice.

1. La _____ se _____ Carmen.

2. El _____ es _____ .

3. El día _____ es _____ .

4. ¿ _____ ?

5. _____ .

Nombre _____

C. Listen carefully to these words. You will hear each word twice. Complete each word by writing **a, e, o,** or **u** on the answer blank. The first one has been done for you. (This test part is optional. Point values should not be applied to students' scores.)

1. g __a__ to

2. p _____ z

3. osc _____ ro

4. _____ so

5. ¿adónd _____ ?

6. v _____ y

7. pl _____ ma

8. vent _____ na

9. sill _____

10. b _____ lígrafo

11. cin _____

Nombre _____

Section 1

A. Look at the pictures in the columns to the right and to the left. Show where you plan to go by drawing a line from each picture to the sentence in the middle that tells where you are going. The first one has been done for you.

1.

2.

   a. Voy a la clase de computadoras.

   b. Voy a la casa.

3.

4.

   c. Voy a la clase de música.

   d. Voy a la clase de arte.

5.

6.

   e. Voy a la biblioteca.

   f. Voy al gimnasio.

UNIDAD 4 / EXAMEN

Nombre _____

B. Read the words in the list. Then look at each picture below and tell what these students are going to do. Write the letter of the word or phrase from the list on the answer blank. The first one has been done for you.

a. pintar	**c.** cantar	**e.** ir al cine
b. practicar los deportes	**d.** estudiar	**f.** usar la computadora

1.

Claudia va a ___**e**___ .

2.

Carlos va a _____ .

3.

Gloria va a _____ .

4.

Diego va a _____ .

5.

Tomás va a _____ .

6.

Víctor va a _____ .

¡HOLA!

Nombre _____

C. Read the sentences. Complete the question after each sentence with an activity. The first one has been done for you.

1. Voy al salón de clase.

   ¿Vas a __ir a la escuela_____ ?

2. Voy al gimnasio.

   ¿Vas a _____ ?

3. Voy a la clase de computadoras.

   ¿Vas a _____ ?

4. Voy a la clase de música.

   ¿Vas a _____ ?

5. Voy a la clase de arte.

   ¿Vas a _____ ?

6. Voy a la biblioteca.

   ¿Vas a _____ ?

Nombre _____

Section 2

A. Look at the pictures below. Then complete the sentences to tell what you or your friends do. Use the verbs shown in parentheses.

M

__**Estudio**__ mucho.
(estudiar)

1.

Iris _____ .
(cantar)

2.

_____ muy bien.
(pintar)

3.

Ana _____ bien.
(pintar)

4.

_____ mucho.
(estudiar)

5.

Luis _____ mucho.
(estudiar)

6.

_____ en la clase.
(cantar)

¡HOLA!

Nombre _____

B. Complete these sentences to tell what you and your friends will do tomorrow.

Hoy	**Mañana**
M Canto	**Voy a cantar** _____ .
1. Estudias.	_____ .
2. Pinto.	_____ .
3. Luis practica los deportes.	Luis _____ los deportes.
4. Usas la computadora.	_____ la computadora.
5. Samuel canta.	Samuel _____ .
6. Estudio.	_____ .
7. Pintas bien.	_____ bien.

Nombre _____

★ **C.** For extra credit, read and answer these questions. Write your answers below in the order shown, and you will have a short paragraph.

1. ¿Qué día es hoy?

2. ¿Adónde vas hoy?

3. ¿Qué vas a hacer?

4. ¿Qué día es mañana?

5. ¿Qué vas a hacer mañana?

1. _____

2. _____

3. _____

4. _____

5. _____

Nombre _____

Section 3

A. Listen to the conversation between Teresa and Pablo. Then you will hear five multiple-choice statements about their conversation. You will hear each statement twice. Circle the letter of the phrase that best completes each statement.

1. a   b   c   4. a   b   c

2. a   b   c   5. a   b   c

3. a   b   c

B. Dictado. Listen carefully to these sentences. You will hear each sentence twice. Write the missing words on the answer blanks.

1. ¿Pintas _____ _____ ?

2. ¿ _____ en la _____ de música?

3. Norma _____ la _____ .

4. Pablo _____ a _____ .

5. Voy a _____ al _____ .

Nombre _____

★ **C.** Now try writing these sentences for extra credit. You will hear each sentence twice.

1. _____

2. _____

3. _____

4. _____

5. _____

D. You will hear a number and a word. If the word contains an **i** sound, circle the number. If the word does not have an **i** sound, do not circle the number. The first two have been done for you. (This test part is optional. Point values should not be applied to students' scores.)

1. (escuela)	4.	7.	10.
2. (pintas)	5.	8.	11.
3.	6.	9.	12.

Nombre _____

Section 1

A. **Las estaciones.** Read the names of the seasons. Then look at the pictures. Under each picture, write the name of the season it shows. Be careful! They are not in order!

el invierno	el verano	el otoño	la primavera

1.

_____

2.

_____

3.

_____

4.

_____

Nombre _____

B. Describe the weather! Look at each picture. Then choose a sentence from the list that describes the picture. Write the letter of the sentence on the answer blank.

a. Hace buen tiempo.		**f.** Hace fresco.	
b. Hace mal tiempo.		**g.** Está nublado.	
c. Hace calor.		**h.** Está nevando.	
d. Hace frío.		**i.** Está lloviendo.	
e. Hace viento.		**j.** Hace sol.	

M

a _____

1.
_____

2.
_____

3.
_____

4.
_____

5.
_____

6.
_____

7.
_____

8.
_____

¡HOLA!

Nombre _____

C. Which season is it? Read the statements below. Respond by circling the name of the season they probably describe.

M Mañana es el primer
día de clases.   (el otoño)   la primavera

1. Está nevando.
   Hace mucho frío.   el invierno   la primavera

2. Hace buen tiempo.
   Un pájaro canta.   el invierno   la primavera

3. Está lloviendo.
   Hace fresco y viento.
   No hay pájaros.   el verano   el otoño

Nombre _____

Section 2

A. Complete these conversations by writing **me, te,** or **le**. The first one has been done for you.

1. ¿Te gusta la primavera?

   Sí, _____**me**_____ gusta.

2. ¿A Sara le gusta el invierno?

   No, a Sara no _____ gusta.

3. ¿ _____ gusta la clase de arte?

   Sí, me gusta.

4. ¿ _____ gusta la casa blanca?

   No, no me gusta.

5. ¿A Carlos _____ gusta estudiar en casa?

   Sí, le gusta estudiar mucho.

6. ¿Te gusta ir al cine?

   Sí, _____ gusta mucho.

Nombre _____

B. Each of these questions and answers contains one word that is not needed. Cross out the extra words.

M ¿Cuál te gusta, el tigre grande o el ~~tigre~~ pequeño?

Me gusta el ~~tigre~~ pequeño.

1. ¿Te gusta la computadora grande o la computadora pequeña?

Me gusta la computadora grande.

2. ¿Cuál te gusta, la biblioteca grande o la biblioteca pequeña?

Me gusta la biblioteca pequeña.

3. ¿Te gusta el gato blanco o el gato gris?

Me gusta el gato gris.

4. ¿Te gusta la bandera verde o la bandera azul?

Me gusta la bandera azul.

5. ¿Cuál te gusta más, el perro amarillo o el perro negro?

Me gusta más el perro negro.

6. ¿Cuál te gusta más, la pluma roja o la pluma amarilla?

Me gusta más la pluma roja.

Nombre _____

C. Like it, or not? Read each question. Look at the face to find out if the answer is **sí** or **no**. Write the answer on the blank.

M ¿A Juan le gusta el otoño?

No, no le gusta.
_____ .

1. ¿A Cecilia le gusta el invierno?

_____ .

2. ¿A Mónica le gusta la primavera?

_____ .

3. ¿A Fernando le gusta la casa?

_____ .

★ **D.** For extra credit, write three sentences in Spanish, telling about things you like, and two sentences, telling about things you do not like.

1. _____

2. _____

3. _____

4. No _____

5. No _____

Nombre _____

Section 3

A. Listen to the conversation between Fernando and Daniel. Then you will hear five multiple-choice statements about their conversation. You will hear each statement twice. Circle the letter of the phrase that best completes each statement.

1. a   b   c   4. a   b   c

2. a   b   c   5. a   b   c

3. a   b   c

B. **Dictado.** Listen carefully to these sentences. You will hear each sentence twice. Write the missing words on the answer blanks.

1. Hay _____ mesa _____ .

2. ¿ _____ luces _____ hay?

3. A Paula le _____ .

4. Hace _____ en el _____ .

5. Hace frío y _____ .

Nombre _____

★ **C.** Now try writing these sentences for extra credit. You will hear each
sentence twice.

1. _____

2. _____

3. _____

4. _____

5. _____

D. Listen carefully. Then complete the words by writing **a, e, i, o,** or **u** in the
blanks. You will hear each word twice. The first two have been done for
you. (This test part is optional. Point values should not be applied to
students' scores.)

1. __e__ stación 4. inviern ____ 7. hac ____ 10. fresc ____

2. n __a__ cer 5. pr ____ mavera 8. of ____ cina 11. est ____ dio

3. g ____ sta 6. ll ____ via 9. nunc ____ 12. c ____ lor

Nombre _____

Section 1

A. Look at the pictures. Then, in the list below, find the name of the month that goes with each picture. Write the letter on the answer blank. The first one has been done for you.

a. enero	**d.** abril	**g.** julio	**j.** octubre
b. febrero	**e.** mayo	**h.** agosto	**k.** noviembre
c. marzo	**f.** junio	**i.** septiembre	**l.** diciembre

1.  __e__

2.  __

3.  __

4.  __

5.  __

6.  __

7.  __

8.  __

9.  __

10.  __

11.  __

12.  __

Nombre _____

B. **¿Qué te gusta hacer?** Imagine that you are the person in each picture. Complete the sentences to tell what you like to do. Use the words below.

| bailar | patinar | caminar | pintar | nadar |

M

Me gusta _____pintar_____ .

1.

Me gusta _____ .

2.

Me gusta _____ .

3.

Me gusta _____ .

4.

Me gusta _____ .

Nombre _____

Section 2

A. Look at the pictures. Then choose the word from the lists below that completes each sentence: The first one has been done for you.

camina	nada	baila
estudia	patina	pinta

1.

Elena **patina** _____ bien.

2.

Luis _____ mucho.

3.

Rita _____ muy bien.

4.

Víctor _____ muy bien.

5.

Laura _____ muy bien.

6.

Inés _____ mucho.

Nombre _____

B. Use the words below to complete the conversation. You will use some words more than once. The first one has been done for you.

yo	tú	él	ella	usted

JUAN: ¿ __**Tú**__ bailas bien?

MARÍA: ¿Yo? Sí, _____ bailo muy bien.

JUAN: ¿Miguel baila bien?

MARÍA: No, _____ no baila bien.

JUAN: ¿Mariela baila mucho?

MARÍA: Sí, _____ baila mucho.

JUAN: Señor Rivas, ¿ _____ baila?

SR. RIVAS: Sí, _____ bailo mucho.

JUAN: ¿Usted baila en casa?

SR. RIVAS: No, _____ no bailo en casa.

JUAN: ¿Canta _____ ?

SR. RIVAS: Sí, _____ canto.

MARÍA: ¿Canta la señora Rivas?

SR. RIVAS: Sí, _____ canta bien.

MARÍA: ¿Canta Alicia?

SR. RIVAS: No, _____ no canta.

¡HOLA!

Nombre _____

C. Read the statements below. Respond to each statement by circling **SIEMPRE, A VECES,** or **NUNCA.**

M Hace buen tiempo	SIEMPRE	(A VECES)	NUNCA
1. Los osos son grandes.	SIEMPRE	A VECES	NUNCA
2. El tigre es un animal.	SIEMPRE	A VECES	NUNCA
3. El perro es un pájaro.	SIEMPRE	A VECES	NUNCA
4. Nado en el salón de clase.	SIEMPRE	A VECES	NUNCA
5. Hay libros en la biblioteca.	SIEMPRE	A VECES	NUNCA

Nombre _____

★ **D.**   For extra credit, complete the answers to the following questions.

[M] ¿Quién nada?

Ella ___**nada**___ .

1. ¿Quién pinta?

Yo _____ .

2. ¿Quién nada?

Él _____ .

3. ¿Quién baila bien?

Tú _____ bien.

4. ¿Quién patina?

Ella _____ .

5. ¿Quién camina mucho?

Usted _____ mucho.

Nombre _____

Section 3

A. Listen to the conversation between Ernesto and Clarita. Then you will hear five statements about their conversation. You will hear each statement twice. Circle **CIERTO** if the statement is true. Circle **FALSO** if it is false.

1.   CIERTO   FALSO

2.   CIERTO   FALSO

3.   CIERTO   FALSO

4.   CIERTO   FALSO

5.   CIERTO   FALSO

B.   Dictado. Listen and write the missing words. You will hear each sentence twice.

1. ¿_____ gusta _____?

2. _____,_____ gusta.

3. ¿Nadas _____ en _____?

4. No. _____ en _____.

5. ¿_____ haces en _____?

Nombre _____

C. Now try writing these sentences for extra credit. You will hear each sentence twice.

1. _____

2. _____

3. _____

4. _____

5. _____

D. Listen carefully to the following twelve words. You will hear each word twice. Complete each word by writing **a** or **e** on the answer blank. The first two have been done for you. (This test part is optional. Point values should not be applied to students' scores.)

1. m __a__ rzo   4. ____ gosto   7. diciembr ____   10. s ____ ptiembre

2. __e__ nero   5. p ____ tinar   8. c ____ minar   11. bail ____ r

3. t ____   6. hac ____   9. n ____ dar   12. v ____ rano

Nombre _____

Section 1

A. Look at the picture. Then, in the list below, find the word that completes the sentence under the picture. The first one has been done for you.

arte	casa	diciembre
biblioteca	computadoras	invierno

1.

Es el mes de __diciembre__ .

2.

Es _____ .
Hace frío.

3.

Es la clase de _____ .

4.

Voy a la clase de

_____ .

5.

Voy a la

_____ .

6.

Voy a la _____ .

Nombre _____

B. Look at the picture. Then write the word that completes the sentence under the picture. The first one has been done for you.

1.

Luis va a _____pintar_____ .

2.

Ana va a _____ .

3.

Hace _____ .

4.

Está _____ .

5.

Me gusta _____ .

6.

Me gusta _____ .

¡HOLA!

Nombre _____

Section 2

A. Circle the word that completes each of these sentences. The first one has been done for you.

1. Ana (canto, cantas, (canta)) bien.

2. A Carlos (me, te, le) gusta el verano.

3. Voy (al, a la) biblioteca.

4. ¿Quién va (al, a la) cine?

5. Yo (estudio, estudias, estudia) mucho.

6. Los domingos, (siempre, a veces, nunca) voy a las clases.

B. Complete these sentences to tell what you and your classmates are going to do tomorrow. The first one has been done for you.

Hoy	**Mañana**
1. Pinto.	_____Voy_____ a pintar.
2. Juan canta.	Juan _____ a cantar.
3. Estudio.	_____ a estudiar.
4. Practicas los deportes.	_____ a practicar los deportes.
5. Pintas bien.	_____ a pintar bien.
6. Anita usa la computadora.	Anita _____ a usar la computadora.

Nombre _____

C. Use the words below to complete this conversation. The first two have been done for you.

yo	tú	él	ella	usted

ELENA: ¿ __Tú__ cantas bien?

JORGE: ¿Yo? No, __yo__ no canto.

ELENA: ¿Ana canta bien?

JORGE: Sí, _____ canta muy bien.

ELENA: ¿José canta bien?

JORGE: No, _____ no canta.

ELENA: Señor García, ¿ _____ canta?

SR. GARCÍA: Sí, _____ canto mucho.

ELENA: Señora Borges, ¿ _____ canta?

SRA. BORGES: Sí, me gusta mucho cantar.

Nombre _____

Section 3

A. Listen to the conversation between Mateo and Andrea. Then you will hear five statements about their conversation. You will hear each statement twice. Circle **CIERTO** if the statement is true. Circle **FALSO** if it is false.

1. CIERTO   FALSO

2. CIERTO   FALSO

3. CIERTO   FALSO

4. CIERTO   FALSO

5. CIERTO   FALSO

B. Dictado. Listen carefully to these sentences. You will hear each sentence twice. Write the missing words on the answer blanks.

1. A Norma _____ gusta _____ .

2. _____ canta muy bien en la clase de _____ .

3. _____ gusta usar la _____ .

4. _____ .

5. _____ .

Nombre _____

C. Listen carefully to these words. You will hear each word twice. Complete each word by writing **a, e, i, o,** or **u** on the answer blank. The first two have been done for you.

1. cin __e__   4. g ____ sta   7. c ____ sa   10. d ____ ciembre

2. p __i__ ntar   5. s ____ l   8. m ____ cho   11. inviern ____

3. dep ____ rtes   6. pat ____ nar   9. art ____   12. est ____ dio

Nombre _____

Section 1

A. Read the sentences in the list below. Then look at the pictures. Write the letter of each sentence on the answer blank beside the picture it describes. The first one has been done for you.

a.	La mariposa es grande.	**d.**	Es el número cincuenta y tres.
b.	Hace mucho viento.	**e.**	Es una pared.
c.	Es un oso.	**f.**	Es un hombre.

1.  _b_

2.  _____

3. 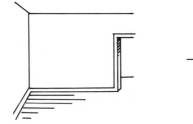 _____

4.  _____

5.  _____

6. **53** _____

Nombre _____

B. First, look at the picture. Then choose the word or phrase from the list that completes the sentence under the picture. Write the word or phrase on the answer blank. The first one has been done for you.

arte   cine   otoño

casa   fin de semana   pintar

1.

Es el

otoño
_____ .

2.

Voy al

_____ .

3.

Carlos va a la

_____ .

4.

sábado	domingo
12	13

Sábado y domingo son el

_____ .

5.

Va a

_____ .

6.

Va a la clase de

_____ .

Nombre _____

C. Look at each picture. Then, on the answer blank, write the word that completes each sentence.

M  Voy a

bailar.

_____

M

enero
?
marzo

Es el mes de

febrero.

_____

1.  Es el

_____

2. Hace

_____

3.  Está

_____

4.  Voy a

_____

5.

julio
?
septiembre

Es el mes de

_____

Nombre _____

Section 2

A. Each sentence below describes **one** person, animal, or thing. Read the sentence. Then, on the answer blank, write the sentence again, changing it to tell about **more than one** person, animal, or thing. The first one has been done for you.

One   **More than one**

1. El loro es verde.   **Los loros son verdes.**
    _____

2. La pared es blanca.   _____

3. El gato es grande.   _____

4. Es un cuaderno.   _____

5. Es una ventana.   _____

6. La mariposa es azul.   _____

Nombre _____

B. Complete these sentences, using words from the list below. The first one has been done for you.

yo	él	usted	te
tú	ella	me	le

1. Señor Vargas, ¿cómo está **usted** ?

2. Clara, ¿ _____ gusta bailar?

3. Sí, _____ gusta bailar.

4. ¿Juan? _____ es mi papá.

5. ¿ _____ pintas bien?

6. A Clara _____ gusta cantar.

7. _____ pinto muy bien.

8. ¿Estudia mucho Isabel?

   Sí, _____ estudia mucho.

MID-YEAR TEST

Nombre _____

C. Complete the sentences below. On each answer blank, write the correct form of the verb in parentheses.

M Clara ____**estudia**____ mucho.
(estudiar)

1. José _____ bien.
(cantar)

2. Iris, ¿ no _____ mucho?
(bailar)

3. El sábado yo _____ a la biblioteca.
(ir)

4. Me _____ el otoño.
(gustar)

5. Daniel _____ casas.
(pintar)

6. Anita _____ muy mal.
(bailar)

7. ¿Adónde _____ tú?
(ir)

8. Yo _____ en casa.
(cantar)

¡HOLA!

Nombre _____

Section 3

A. Listen to the conversation between Ernesto and Clarita. Then you will hear five multiple-choice statements about their conversation. You will hear each statement twice. Circle the letter of the word or words that best complete each statement.

1. a   b   c   4. a   b   c

2. a   b   c   5. a   b   c

3. a   b   c

B. Dictado. Listen carefully to these sentences. You will hear each sentence twice. Write the missing words on the answer blanks.

1. Hay _____ libros en la _____ .

2. ¿ _____ está la alumna?

3. _____ muy buen _____ .

4. _____ .

5. _____ .

Nombre _____

C. Listen carefully to these words. You will hear each word twice. Complete each word by writing **a, e, i, o,** or **u** on the answer blank. The first two have been done for you. (This test part is optional. Point values should not be applied to students' scores.)

1. __a__ gosto

2. inviern __o__

3. hac _____

4. osc _____ ro

5. larg _____

6. dom _____ ngo

7. músic _____

8. az _____ l

9. _____ sta

10. g _____ mnasio

11. may _____

12. pl _____ ma

Nombre _____

Section 1

A. **¿Qué tienes?** Read the words in the list. Then look at each picture below. Imagine that you are the person in the picture and complete each sentence using a word from the list. The first one has been done for you.

calor	frío	hambre
prisa	sueño	sed

1.

   Tengo ____**sed**____ .

2.

   Tengo _____ .

3.

   Tengo _____ .

4.

   Tengo _____ .

5.

   Tengo _____ .

6.

   Tengo _____ .

Nombre _____

B. Look at each picture below. Write a sentence to tell what each person is saying. The first one has been done for you.

1. **Tengo suerte.** _____

_____

2. _____

_____

3. _____

_____

4. _____

_____

5. _____

_____

6.
$$\begin{array}{r} 5 \\ \times 5 \\ \hline 25 \end{array}$$
$$\begin{array}{r} 5 \\ \times 5 \\ \hline 30 \end{array}$$
_____

_____

C. Imagine that someone asks your age. Write the question you would be asked in Spanish. Then write your answer.

¿ _____ ?

Tengo _____ .

Nombre _____

Section 2

A. Complete these sentences, using **tengo, tienes,** or **tiene.**

M Humberto ____**tiene**____ calor.

1. El señor Ortiz _____ suerte.

2. Yo no _____ suerte.

3. Sandra, ¿tú _____ sed?

4. No, yo _____ sueño.

5. Rogelio, ¿qué _____ tú?

6. Yo _____ tres canarios.

B. Tell whether the speaker would use **tú** or **usted** in each of these situations. The first one has been done for you.

1. You are speaking to an older person. _____**usted**_____

2. You are speaking to a friend your age. _____

3. You are speaking to a visiting teacher. _____

4. You are speaking to a visiting student about your age. _____

5. You are speaking to your brother. _____

6. An adult is speaking to you. _____

7. An adult is speaking to another adult. _____

8. A little girl is speaking to her sister. _____

Nombre _____

C. Complete these sentences by writing either **tú** or **usted**.

[M] Señor Ortiz, ____usted____ tiene la gripe.

1. Señor Ibarra, ¿cuántos años tiene _____?

2. Rosa, _____ tienes razón.

3. Claudia, _____ tienes sueño.

4. Señora Prado, ¿cómo está _____ ?

5. Nicolás, _____ no tienes prisa.

6. Leonardo, _____ tienes suerte.

7. Señorita García, _____ tiene sueño.

Nombre _____

★ **D.** For extra credit, complete the questions for these answers.

M ¿Enrique ____**tiene**____ razón?

No, él no tiene razón.

1. ¿Quién _____ calor?

Yo no. Yo tengo frío.

2. Eduardo, ¿tú _____ frío?

Sí, tengo mucho frío.

3. ¿Tú _____ la gripe?

Sí, tengo la gripe.

4. ¿Cuántos años _____ don Ernesto?

Tiene noventa años.

5. ¿Cuántos años _____ yo?

Tienes diez años.

Nombre _____

Section 3

A. Listen to the conversation between Dora, Adela, and Arturo. Then you will hear five statements about their conversation. You will hear each statement twice. Circle **CIERTO** if the statement is true. Circle **FALSO** if it is false.

1.   CIERTO   FALSO

2.   CIERTO   FALSO

3.   CIERTO   FALSO

4.   CIERTO   FALSO

5.   CIERTO   FALSO

B.   Dictado. Listen, and then write the missing words. You will hear each sentence twice.

1. ¿ _____ años tiene la _____ Cortez?

2. ¿ _____? Tiene _____ años.

3. ¿ _____ gusta la _____?

4. _____, le gusta mucho _____.

5. _____ tiene muchos _____.

Nombre _____

★**C.** Now try writing these sentences for extra credit. You will hear each sentence twice.

1. _____

2. _____

3. _____

4. _____

5. _____

D. Listen carefully to these twelve words. You will hear each word twice. Complete each word by writing **e** or **i** on the answer blank. The first two have been done for you. (This test part is optional. Point values should not be applied to students' scores.)

1. l __e__ che   4. v ____ mos   7. pr ____ sa   10. herv ____ da

2. c __i__ nco   5. p ____ so   8. s ____ d   11. tr ____ s

3. v ____ ven   6. p ____ so   9. gr ____ pe   12. suert ____

Nombre _____

Section 1

A. Look at each picture. Then choose a phrase from the list to show the time of day, and write it on the answer blank. The first one has been done for you.

---

el mediodía   la salida del sol

la medianoche   la puesta del sol

---

1.    2.    3.    4.

1. Es   **la salida del sol** _____ .

2. Es   _____ .

3. Es   _____ .

4. Es   _____ .

Nombre _____

B.   Tell how much time is shown on the clock. The first one has been done for you.

1.    **un minuto** _____
_____

2. 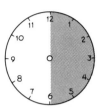   _____
_____

3. 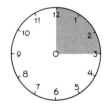   _____
_____

4.    _____
_____

C.   Look at Mónica's schedule. Then finish the sentences that tell where she is at different times of the day. The first one has been done for you.

Mónica	
7:30 a.m.	la escuela
8:00 a.m.	la clase de música
5:10 p.m.	el cine
9:20 p.m.	la casa

1.   A las siete y media de _____**la mañana**_____ Mónica va a la escuela.

2.   A las ocho en _____ tiene la clase de música.

3.   A las cinco y diez de _____ va al cine.

4.   A las nueve y veinte de _____ va a la casa.

Nombre _____

D. Use a question word from the list to complete the conversation below. The first one has been done for you.

Adónde	Cuál	Cuántos	Quién
Cómo	Cuándo	Qué	

1. P: ¿ __**Cómo**__ te llamas?
   R: Me llamo Juan López.

2. P: ¿ _____ años tienes?
   R: Tengo doce años.

3. P: ¿ _____ vas a las ocho de la mañana?
   R: Voy a la clase de computadoras.

4. P: ¿ _____ es la profesora?
   R: Es la señora Gómez.

5. P: ¿ _____ clase tienes a las nueve de la mañana?
   R: Tengo la clase de arte.

6. P: ¿ _____ tienes la clase de música?
   R: A las diez de la mañana.

7. P: ¿ _____ es tu clase favorita?
   R: Es la clase de arte.

Nombre _____

Section 2

A. Look at each clock. Then read the words in the list. Use words from the list to complete the sentences beside the clocks. The first one has been done for you.

es	son	y	menos

1.  **Es** _____ la una

   y _____ diez.

2. 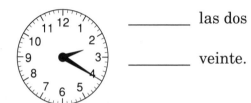 _____ las dos

   _____ veinte.

3.  _____ las tres

   _____ veinte.

4. 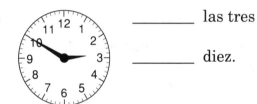 _____ las tres

   _____ diez.

5.  _____ la una

   _____ cuarto.

6.  _____ las cuatro

   _____ media.

7.  _____ las

   cinco _____

   cuarto.

8.  _____ las

   cinco _____

   cinco.

9.  _____ la una

   _____ cinco.

¡HOLA!

Nombre _____

B. Circle the word that completes each question. The first one has been done for you.

1. ¿ ((Cómo) , Qué) está usted?

2. ¿ (Quién , Qué) hora es?

3. ¿ (Adónde , Cuál) es tu número de teléfono?

4. ¿ (Adónde , Cuántos) va usted?

5. ¿De (qué , cuándo) color es el canario?

6. ¿ (Cuándo , Cuántos) alumnos hay en la clase?

7. ¿ (Cuándo , Cuántos) patinas?

8. ¿ (Quién , Cómo) tiene sed?

Nombre _____

c. Write sentences that tell the time shown on these digital watches. The first one has been done for you.

1.

10:12   **Son las diez y doce.** _____

2.

9:20   _____

3.

7:45   _____

4.

5:10   _____

5.

3:55   _____

6.

1:30   _____

Nombre _____

★ **D.**   Now answer these questions for extra credit.

1.   ¿Qué hora es?

_____

2.   ¿A qué hora vas a la escuela?

_____

3.   ¿A qué hora tienes la clase de español?

_____

4.   ¿Cuál es tu clase favorita?

_____

5.   ¿Cuándo vas a casa?

_____

Nombre _____

Section 3

A. Listen to the conversation between Mónica, Pedro, and Pedro's mother. Then you will hear five statements about their conversation. You will hear each statement twice. Circle **CIERTO** if the statement is true. Circle **FALSO** if it is false.

1.   CIERTO   FALSO

2.   CIERTO   FALSO

3.   CIERTO   FALSO

4.   CIERTO   FALSO

5.   CIERTO   FALSO

B.   Dictado. Listen carefully to these sentences. You will hear each sentence twice. Write the missing words on the answer blanks.

1. José _____ a la escuela a las _____ de la mañana.

2. A José _____ gusta _____ .

3. A las _____ en _____ , José va a la casa.

4. En casa, José _____ dos _____ .

5. José estudia a las _____ de la _____ .

Nombre _____

★ **C.** Now try writing these sentences for extra credit. You will hear each sentence twice.

1. _____

2. _____

3. _____

4. _____

5. _____

D. Listen carefully to the following twelve words. You will hear each word twice. Complete each word by writing **o** or **u** on the answer blank. The first two have been done for you. (This test part is optional. Point values should not be applied to students' scores.)

1. h __o__ ra

2. min __u__ to

3. cuart _____

4. _____ na

5. p _____ nto

6. s _____ l

7. m _____ la

8. n _____ che

9. ¿cuánd _____ ?

10. ¿c _____ mo?

11. g _____ sta

12. m _____ cho

Nombre _____

Section 1

A. Sara studies eight school subjects. Look at each picture. Then choose the word from the list that names the subject. Write the letter on the answer blank. The first one has been done for you.

a. ciencias	**c.** matemáticas	**e.** inglés	**g.** salud
b. geografía	**d.** español	**f.** ciencias sociales	**h.** educación física

1.    **h**

2.  book   _____

3.    _____

4.    _____

5.  libro   _____

6.    _____

7.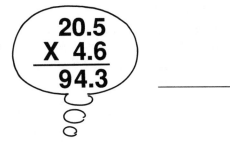

20.5
X 4.6
94.3   _____

8.    _____

Nombre _____

B. Imagine what the students in the pictures below would be saying. Then choose a word from the list and write a sentence. Be sure to check your spelling! The first one has been done for you.

aburrido	divertido	fantástico	interesante
difícil	fácil	importante	terrible

1.    <u>**Es divertido**</u>

    _____ .

2.    _____

    _____ .

3. 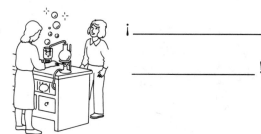   _____

    _____ .

4.    ¡_____

    _____ !

5.    ¡_____

    _____ !

6.    _____

    _____ .

7.    _____

    _____ .

8. _____

    _____ .

Nombre _____

C. On the answer blank, write the question that is missing from this conversation.

ELENA: Me gusta la clase de español.

DANIEL: _____

ELENA: El español es muy importante y divertido.

UNIDAD 9 / EXAMEN

Nombre _____

Section 2

A. Find out what subjects Alicia likes. Complete each sentence below using **gusta** or **gustan**. The first one has been done for you.

ALICIA: Me ____**gustan**____ las ciencias sociales.

CARLOS: ¿Te _____ las matemáticas?

ALICIA: Sí, y me _____ las ciencias.

CARLOS: ¿Te _____ la educación física?

ALICIA: No, no me _____ los deportes.

B. Make it clear who likes dogs and cats and who does not like them. First, read the conversations below. Then, from the list, choose phrases to complete the conversation and write them on the answer blanks. The first one has been done for you.

no me gustan	me gusta	me gustan
te gustan	no me gusta	le gustan

SAMUEL: Señor Martí, ¿ ____**le gustan**____ los perros?

SR. MARTÍ: No, _____ los perros. Los gatos, sí.

_____ los gatos.

JUANITA: Samuel, ¿ _____ los gatos?

SAMUEL: No. Alicia tiene un gato. _____ los gatos.

JUANITA: Pues, yo también tengo un gato. Se llama Dot.

_____ mucho Dot.

¡HOLA!

Nombre _____

C. Find out what these people do. Complete their conversations by writing the correct form of the verb shown in parentheses above each conversation. The first one has been done for you.

(leer)

1. LUIS: Yo _____leo_____ español.

   ANA: Tú _____ inglés, ¿no?

   LUIS: Sí. Mi amigo Daniel _____ inglés y español.

(aprender)

2. JULIO: ¿Qué _____ Ana en la clase de ciencias?

   ANITA: Ella _____ mucho en la clase de ciencias.

   JULIO: ¿Qué _____ tú en la clase de matemáticas?

(escribir)

3. JOSÉ: Alejandro _____ bien.

   HUGO: José, ¿tú _____ bien?

   JOSÉ: Sí, yo _____ bien.

(comprender)

4. DIANA: Yo no _____ a Carlos.

   PACO: Carlos no _____ a Sara.

   DIANA: Tú no _____ a Carlos.

Nombre _____

★ **D.** For extra credit, complete this conversation. Write the correct form of each verb in parentheses. The first one has been done for you.

SARA: Yo no ___**aprendo**___ mucho en la clase de inglés.

No _____ (comprender) al profesor.

ROSA: ¡Qué lástima! ¿ _____ (leer) tú el libro?

SARA: Sí, _____ (leer) el libro y _____ (escribir)

mucho. Voy a hablar con el profesor.

ROSA: Buena idea. Él va a _____ (comprender).

Nombre _____

Section 3

A. Listen to the conversation between Alejandro and señor López. Then you will hear five statements about their conversation. You will hear each statement twice. Circle **CIERTO** if the statement is true. Circle **FALSO** if it is false.

1.   CIERTO   FALSO

2.   CIERTO   FALSO

3.   CIERTO   FALSO

4.   CIERTO   FALSO

5.   CIERTO   FALSO

B. **Dictado.** Listen carefully and write the missing words. You will hear each sentence twice.

1. _____ mucho en la _____ .

2. _____ profesores son _____ .

3. Las clases son _____ interesantes.

4. _____ dos clases _____ .

5. Son las clases de _____ y de matemáticas.

6. No me _____ la clase de educación _____ .

Nombre _____

★ **C.** Now try writing these phrases and sentences for extra credit. You will hear each one twice.

1. _____

2. _____

3. _____

4. _____

5. _____

D. Listen carefully to the thirteen words that follow. You will hear each word twice. If you hear the consonant **d** in a word, circle **sí**. If you do not hear the consonant **d**, circle **no**. The first three have been done for you. (This test part is optional. Point values should not be applied to students' scores.)

1.	(sí)	no	6.	sí	no	11.	sí	no
2.	sí	(no)	7.	sí	no	12.	sí	no
3.	(sí)	no	8.	sí	no	13.	sí	no
4.	sí	no	9.	sí	no			
5.	sí	no	10.	sí	no			

Nombre _____

Section 1

A. A family tree

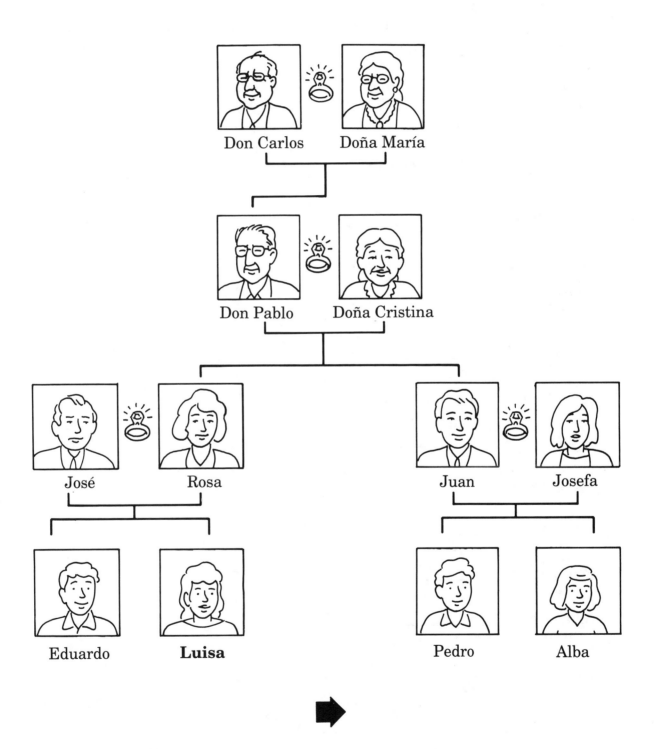

Nombre _____

Part **A**, continued.

Imagine that you are Luisa in the family tree on the previous page. Use words from the list to tell how the following people are related to you. The first one has been done for you.

abuelo	hijo	tío	primo
abuela	hija	tía	prima
bisabuelo	hermano	mamá	
bisabuela	hermana	papá	

1. Don Carlos es mi _____bisabuelo_____ .

2. Doña María es mi _____ .

3. Don Pablo es mi _____ .

4. Doña Cristina es mi _____ .

5. José es mi _____ .

6. Rosa es mi _____ .

7. Juan es mi _____ .

8. Josefa es mi _____ .

9. Eduardo es mi _____ .

10. Pedro es mi _____ .

11. Alba es mi _____ .

Nombre _____

B. Imagine that you are David in the family tree below. Complete the sentences to tell how the following people are related to you. The first one has been done for you.

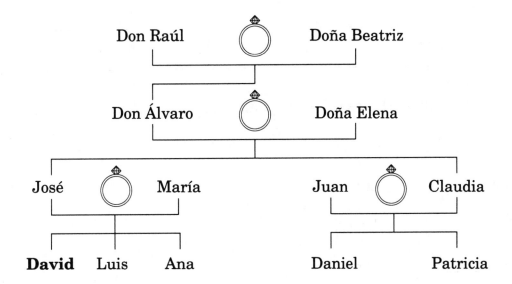

1. Don Raúl y doña Beatriz son mis ___**bisabuelos**___ .

2. Don Álvaro y doña Elena son mis _____ .

3. José y María son mis _____ .

4. Juan y Claudia son mis _____ .

5. Luis y Ana son mis _____ .

6. Daniel y Patricia son mis _____ .

Nombre _____

Section 2

A. Who owns what? Use the words below to fill in the blanks to show who owns the things named. The first one has been done for you.

mi	tu	su	sus	tus	mis

1. First say that these things belong to you:

a. Es _____**mi**_____ casa.

b. Son _____ cuadernos.

c. Son _____ libros.

d. Es _____ perro.

2. Now tell your friend Claudia that these things below to her:

a. Es _____ loro.

b. Es _____ lápiz.

c. Son _____ canarios.

d. Son _____ bolígrafos.

3. Now tell about things that your teacher owns:

a. Es _____ globo.

b. Son _____ mapas.

c. Es _____ escritorio.

d. Son _____ borradores.

Nombre _____

B. Use the endings **-ito, -itos, -ita,** or **-itas** to show that things are small, or that you especially like certain people.

| M | Tengo un <u>carro</u>. | Tengo un ___**carrito**___ . |

¡Hola, <u>primas</u>!   ¡Hola, ___**primitas**___ !

1. Tengo una <u>mesa</u>.   Tengo una _____ .

2. Tengo un <u>globo</u>.   Tengo un _____ .

3. Tengo unos <u>libros</u>.   Tengo unos _____ .

4. Tengo unas <u>casas</u>.   Tengo unas _____ .

5. Tengo un <u>papel</u>.   Tengo un _____ .

6. ¡Hola, <u>abuelo</u>!   ¡Hola, _____ !

7. ¡Hola, <u>hermanos</u>!   ¡Hola, _____ !

8. ¡Hola, <u>hijos</u>!   ¡Hola, _____ !

9. ¡Hola, <u>hermana</u>!   ¡Hola, _____ !

★ **C.** Now for extra credit, add endings that make nicknames of these five Spanish names.

1. Ana _____   4. Sara _____

2. Juan _____   5. Rosa _____

3. Ricardo _____

Nombre _____

Section 3

A. Listen to the conversation between Luisa and Eduardo. Then you will hear five statements about their conversation. You will hear each statement twice. Circle **CIERTO** if the statement is true. Circle **FALSO** if it is false.

1. CIERTO   FALSO

2. CIERTO   FALSO

3. CIERTO   FALSO

4. CIERTO   FALSO

5. CIERTO   FALSO

B. Dictado. Listen and write the missing words. You will hear each sentence twice.

1. ¿ _____ se llama la _____ de Carlos?

2. Se llama Mercedes. _____ _____ años.

3. ¿Cuántos _____ _____ en la familia de Carlos?

4. Hay _____ : Carlos, Eduardo _____ Mercedes.

5. _____ familia no es muy _____ .

Nombre _____

★ **C.** Now try writing these sentences for extra credit. You will hear each sentence twice.

ROSITA: _____

JUAN: _____

ROSITA: _____

JUAN: _____

ROSITA: _____

D. Listen carefully to these twelve words. You will hear each word twice. Complete each word by writing **p** or **t** on the answer blank. The first two have been done for you. (This test part is optional. Point values should not be applied to students' scores.)

1. ro __p__ a

2. ro __t__ a

3. ga ____ o

4. sa ____ o

5. ____ risa

6. ____ arde

7. es ____ añol

8. ____ ío

9. his ____ oria

10. ____ orque

11. diver ____ ido

12. ____ atino

Nombre _____

Section 1

A. Read the sentences in the lists below. Then look at the pictures. Write the letter of each sentence on the answer blank beside the picture it describes. The first one has been done for you.

a. Está nevando.

b. Es una mujer.

c. ¿Qué día es hoy?

d. El mes es febrero.

e. Tengo mucho calor.

f. Son las tres y media.

1.  b

2. 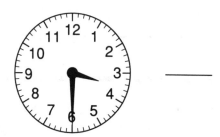 ___

3. **martes** ___

4.  ___

5.  ___

6.  ___

¡HOLA!

Nombre _____

B. First, look at the picture. Then choose the word from the list that completes the sentence under the picture. Write the word on the answer blank. The first one has been done for you.

bandera	fácil	abuelos
estudiar	rosado	viento

1.

Hace _____viento_____ .

2.

Es una _____ .

3.

El flamenco es

_____ .

4.

Voy a _____ .

5.

Es _____ .

6.

Son mis _____ .

END-OF-YEAR TEST

Nombre _____

C. Look at each picture. Then, on the answer blank, write the word that completes the phrase or sentence. The first one has been done for you.

1.

   El canario es ___amarillo___ .

2.

   Practico los deportes en el _____ .

3.

   Él tiene _____ .

4.

   Es la una menos _____ .

5.

   Es el número _____ .

6.

   Es el número _____ .

¡HOLA!

Nombre _____

Section 2

A. Each sentence below describes one person, animal, or thing. Read the sentence. Then, on the answer blank, write the sentence again, changing it to tell about more than one person, animal, or thing. The first one has been done for you.

One   **More than one**

Los osos son blancos.

1. El oso es blanco.   _____

_____

2. El borrador es pequeño.   _____

_____

3. La bandera es roja.   _____

_____

4. Es un globo interesante.   _____

_____

5. Es una ventana grande.   _____

_____

6. Mi prima es divertida.   _____

_____

END-OF-YEAR TEST

Nombre _____

B. Complete these sentences using words from the list below. The first one has been done for you.

yo	él	usted	te	mis
tú	ella	me	le	su

1. Ana, ¿ ___**tú**___ hablas inglés?

2. _____ bailo muy mal.

3. Señor Gómez, ¿adónde va _____ ?

4. Yo, no. No _____ gustan los animales.

5. A Juanita _____ gusta el pájaro blanco.

6. Me gusta mucho la casa de mi abuela. ¡ _____ casa es fantástica!

7. ¿Nada bien Fernando?

   Sí, _____ nada muy bien.

8. Mi mamá tiene dos hijas. Ellas son _____ hermanas.

Nombre _____

C. Complete the sentences below. On each answer blank, write the correct form of the verb in parentheses.

M Anita ____**baila**____ mucho.
(bailar)

1. Carlos _____ en casa.
(estudiar)

2. Yo _____ mucho en mis clases.
(aprender)

3. Ernesto, ¿por qué no _____ en español?
(escribir)

4. ¿Ellos _____ tus primos?
(ser)

5. ¿Cuántos años _____ Diego?
(tener)

6. A Jaime le _____ los ratones.
(gustar)

7. María _____ a cantar.
(ir)

8. ¿Tú _____ muchos libros?
(leer)

Nombre _____

Section 3

A. Listen to the conversation between Luis and Ana. Then you will hear five multiple-choice statements about their conversation. You will hear each statement twice. Circle the letter of the word or words that best completes each statement.

1. a   b   c   4. a   b   c

2. a   b   c   5. a   b   c

3. a   b   c

B. Dictado. Listen carefully to these sentences. You will hear each sentence twice. Write the missing words on the answer blanks.

1. El _____ se _____ David.

2. ¿_____ _____ David?

3. _____ va a sus _____ favoritas.

4. _____

5. _____

Nombre _____

C. Listen carefully to these words. You will hear each word twice. Complete each word by writing a vowel or consonant letter on the answer blank. The first two have been done for you. (This test part is optional. Point values should not be applied to students' scores.)

1. pr __i__ ma

2. pier __n__ a

3. a _____ rigo

4. me _____ ianoche

5. r _____ bio

6. c _____ mica

7. jue _____ es

8. qu _____

9. ma _____ ana

10. za _____ atos

11. l _____ cio

12. cin _____ ura

Teacher's Notes

Teacher's Notes

Teacher's Notes

Teacher's Notes